The
PERFECT
LETTER

JOAN MINNINGER, Ph.D.

THE
PERFECT
LETTER

MAINSTREET BOOKS / DOUBLEDAY

NEW YORK   LONDON   TORONTO   SYDNEY   AUCKLAND

A Main Street Book

PUBLISHED BY DOUBLEDAY

a division of Bantam Doubleday Dell Publishing Group, Inc.
1540 Broadway, New York, New York 10036

MAIN STREET BOOKS, DOUBLEDAY, and the portrayal of a
building with a tree are trademarks of Doubleday, a
division of Bantam Doubleday Dell Publishing Group, Inc.

Excerpts from *Effective Business Writing Newsletter*, copyrighted
and published by The Economics Press, Inc., Fairfield,
New Jersey, copyright © 1991.

LIBRARY OF CONGRESS CATALOGING-IN-PUBLICATION DATA

Minninger, Joan.
　The perfect letter / Joan Minninger.—1st ed.
　　p.　cm.
　1. Commercial correspondence.　2. Business writing.　3. Letter-
writing.　I. Title.
HF5721.M56　1992
651.7'5—dc20　　　　　　　　　　　　　　　　　91-9037
　　　　　　　　　　　　　　　　　　　　　　　　　　CIP

ISBN 0-385-41998-8
Copyright © 1992 by Joan Minninger, Ph.D.

BOOK DESIGN BY PATRICE FODERO

To Delos,
who invented the rewrite

Acknowledgments

The Perfect Letter is based on original material generously provided by my workshop participants and additional material selected from *Effective Business Writing Newsletter*. Grateful appreciation to Eleanor Knowles Dugan, who brilliantly crafted the lion's share of rewrites. Thanks to Jeanne Glennon and Becky Gordon for their superb editorial help. To Dr. Barbara Sanner, this book's godmother, who provided personal support from the beginning. And finally to my agent Michael Larsen and editor John Duff, with whom it is a continuing pleasure to work.

Contents

What You Need to Start Writing

CHAPTER 1

About Letters

The purpose of this book is to show you how to write powerful, effective business letters. In good times, Perfect Letters are a get-ahead tool. In hard times they are an essential survival skill. Employees who can prove they are income-producing assets to their companies are the last to go. Small-business owners who handle correspondence in a big-business way have an automatic edge over competitors. Perfect Letters are not only good business, they may be the difference between business and no business.

Anyone can learn to write Perfect Letters—letters that persuade, motivate, soothe, or convey complex information clearly and concisely. Even better, when you've acquired the basic skills, it takes no more effort to write a Perfect Letter than a poor one. The organizational techniques you'll learn in this book will help you focus your thoughts, end procrastination, and speed your work.

With the Perfect Letter technique, you'll learn to do three things:

1. Write so you can be understood.
2. Write so you can't possibly be *mis*understood.
3. Make each letter you send a valuable asset, not a liability.

It is the possibility of exposure and loss that immobilizes some would-be letter writers. So much can hinge on saying the right thing—or *not* saying the wrong thing—that procrastination results in situations that are far more difficult and costly than any letter, no matter how poorly written, could have created. You'll learn how to end writer's block in "The Two-Step Technique for Perfect Letters" on page 7.

WHAT IS A LETTER?

A letter is any written substitute for face-to-face communication. Like speech, it can convey information in neutral, friendly, casual, formal, hostile, or urgent tones. Like speech, it can also be precise, vague, dramatic, or incomprehensible. Like the spoken word, it can be received gratefully or resentfully, and the response can be brought about by style as well as content.

Letters are often extensions of ourselves and our businesses. They represent us to the world, a part of us revealed and fixed forever on paper. This awesome responsibility produces tension, which in turn can produce letters that sometimes don't convey the intended message or have the desired effect.

THE HIGH COST OF WEAK WRITING

Whenever you think that you don't have time to write a coherent letter, remember that confusing, ineffective, or ill-advised letters are expensive! At best, they waste the time of the reader and can cost you prestige and the reader's good will. At worst, weak letters can lead to expensive mistakes, loss of credibility, and disastrous law suits.

What are the common traps for business letter writers?

Complex Issues

Often letter writers who are wrestling with complex issues follow a traditional once-upon-a-time approach, putting down their thoughts as they occur. They wind up unintentionally concealing their real purpose in writing, by burying it at the end of the letter or leaving it out all together, assuming the reader will guess it.

Emotion-charged Topics

Knowing that a lot depends on the reader's response to a letter can cause anxiety and errors in judgment about the real purpose of writing the letter, what points to cover, and the tone.

Complaints

Letters written in anger are often expensive. That's because they either fail to focus on the real issue, or they address feelings and personalities ("You idiot!") not facts ("My order was late again").

Refusals

How do you say "No!" and not produce an enemy? The normal temptation is to offer several excuses, cite policy, and then put the reader off to a later date, perhaps in a way that obscures the actual refusal. This is at best unkind, at worst damaging to your reputation for fairness and decisiveness.

CLEAR THINKING—A GOAL, NOT A BEGINNING

At this point, most business-writing books will be telling you that you must have a clear idea of what you are going to say before you touch a sheet of paper. You must watch your grammar, your syntax, your tone, your facts. Fortunately for you, that's *not* the Perfect Letter method!

When you write the first draft of an especially difficult letter, start by writing anything you want to write any way you want to write it—rambling, rude, ungrammatical, figuring out as you go what you really think, what you really mean to say and want to say, what you want the reader to do, and what you are willing or able to do in return.

Picasso said, "I paint to show what I found, not what I was looking for." That goes for letters as well as paintings. When you face an especially challenging letter-writing assignment, write to find out what you want to say. Use the exploratory technique to discover what you think, what you know, what you want to happen. You will frequently astound yourself.

This exploratory phase is the first half of the Two-Step Technique for Perfect Letters. In the second half, you go on to craft your letter so it says what your *reader* needs to know, in the way *you* want to say it, so that you are most likely to get the results you want.

CHAPTER 2

The Two-Step Technique for Perfect Letters

The way to organize difficult, emotionally charged, complex, politically strategic, or confusing material is to divide and conquer. Start by dividing your writing (and thinking) into two phases.

WHERE TO START—
THE EXPLORATORY PHASE

Sit down and write (or pace and dictate) your first thoughts and reactions. Many writing instruction books start by telling you that you must think clearly *before* you write. With the Perfect Letter technique, that's not necessary. The two-step technique lets you discover what you think, evaluate it, and then arrange and present it for the convenience of the reader.

Use the most elaborate once-upon-a-time form you wish, to tell everything you know and feel about the subject. Explore every facet. Digress, develop, dazzle. Allow yourself to write whatever comes into your head with no attempt to organize it or censor yourself. Gather all you know that is relevant. Be sure to describe what reaction you'd like your reader to have to this letter.

If you catch yourself editing, if a voice inside you starts nagging with "That's not right," reply like the skilled administrator you are: "Of course, it's not. You're very perceptive to notice. I'll need your skills later to help craft this, so have my secretary pencil you in for four o'clock on your way out.''

Writer's Block

If you can't get started, try any of the following exercises that I use in my Perfect Memo Writing seminars.

"I THINK": Jot any of the phrases below on a sheet of paper and then keep writing.

I know . . .	I will . . .
I think . . .	I won't . . .
I feel . . .	I can . . .
I want . . .	I can't . . .

Change the pronoun to whatever is appropriate: I, you, he, she, we, they.

JUST TEN MINUTES: Set a timer for ten minutes. If you write by hand, put your pen on the paper and draw continuous loops over and over until words come to you—any words. They can be your shopping list or a poem. Very soon, you'll find your real topic intruding and taking over.

If you usually type or word-process your first draft, type *fjfjfj* over and over until words come. If you're using a typewriter, you can insert a roll of shelf paper or continuous computer paper so you're not interrupted by having to put in a new sheet.

Having a ten-minute limit makes it easy to start, and almost no one can stop when the timer goes off.

When you have created the raw material for your difficult letter, go on to the Crafting Phase.

HOW TO FINISH—THE CRAFTING PHASE

Now that you know what you know, what you think, and what you'd like to happen, you're ready to pick out what you want to tell your reader. This is your Crafting Phase.

Step 1: Underline what your reader needs to know.

Go back over what you have written and put a line under everything your reader needs to know. (If you truly believe your reader needs to know that you think s/he's incompetent, dishonest, and stupid, leave that in . . . for now.)

Step 2: Decide why you are writing.

What is the purpose of your letter? Write this down at the top of a sheet of paper:

The purpose of this letter is to _____.

You probably won't start your finished letter with that exact phrase, but it helps get you started.

(This is where you decide whether to use any angry words, whether they help or hinder your purpose. See "Angry Letters," page 35.)

Step 3: Divide what you have underlined into topics.

If your raw material covers more than one point, organize it into categories. If the material is unusually long, you may want to sort it into separate piles or separate temporary word-processor files, labeled by topic.

Step 4: Write a heading for each topic.

Yes, you can use headings in letters. Any letter that covers more than one subject or one page will probably benefit from internal headings. They help you:

LET THE READER SCAN YOUR COMMUNICATION, seeing with a quick glance what you are saying.

PROVIDE AN OVERVIEW and a handy way to retrieve key points later.

GROUP THE INFORMATION INTO LOGICAL CATEGORIES in your exploratory writing, such as:

- what each department or person is expected to do
- alternatives (choose one)
- a series of supports for your conclusion
- a series of steps to be taken
- deadlines and important future dates
- dates in a chronology of what has happened
- topics discussed at meeting
- positive and negative points
- past and future actions

Headings help you as a writer because you are less likely to scatter information on the same subject throughout your letter, to leave out part of a sequence, or to repeat yourself. Use headings whenever your letter covers several facets of one subject, covers more than one subject, or contains secondary information that needs to be highlighted (such as alternatives, changes, new procedures, etc.)

Use accurate, informative headings that let the reader know immediately what you are talking about: Your New Medical Benefits (not Benefits); When to Deliver Parts (not Timetable).

Step 5: Number topics in order of importance to the reader.

What does the reader need to know first? Second? And after that? Put your topics in order of importance. If it is logical, cluster all the things you are asking the reader to do at the beginning of the letter and highlight them clearly by numbering them in sequence or by using bullets. Then continue with general information or background.

Step 6: Write your opening sentence or paragraph.

Put your purpose up front. Why are you writing? Is that clear in the first paragraph?

Your first sentence should always tell your readers why they are reading your letter. Let them know immediately if you want them to act, to decide, or simply to be aware of the information you are sending. Don't make them read and reread, muttering, "Why are you telling me this?"

Summarize your requests, complaints, or suggestions in the first paragraph. Avoid telling a long once-upon-a-time story and then burying your conclusion at the bottom of page two. Your reader may not make it that far.

Step 7: Fill in the gaps.

Follow your opening paragraph with your other topics or paragraphs in order of their importance to the reader. Then read your letter as a whole. Fill in any gaps you see by supplying missing facts, feelings, background information, or supports.

Step 8: Polish.

Smooth your sentences and transitions. Check spelling, grammar, and punctuation. Reread for tone: do you sound as friendly, formal, stern, apologetic, enthusiastic, or efficient as you want to sound? Do your opening words convey both your purpose and your desired tone?

Your Perfect Letter Workbook

CHAPTER 3

How to Use This Book

This book consists of disguised versions of *real* letters, arranged in a "before" and "after" format. Glance at some of the Originals (always on a left-hand page), and imagine your morning mail full of such letters. Would you race through them eagerly, responding positively to their authors' suggestions and requests? Do they have strong visual appeal? Would you even understand all of them? (These misguided gems have been collected during my nineteen years of Executive Writing seminars for Fortune 500 companies.)

The workbook section is divided into eighteen common types of letters, arranged alphabetically for your convenience:

Agreements	Followups
Announcements	Instructions
Angry Letters	Newsletters
Apologies	Notifications
Asking for Action	Promotional Letters
Asking for a Decision	Refusals
Complaints	Response Letters
Condolences	Thank You's
Congratulations	Urgent Notifications

If some of the subjects aren't relevant to your current business writing, it's okay to skip over them, but for each of the subjects you are interetsed in be sure to:

1. Read each Original letter that appears on the left-hand page. Then follow the instructions on the "What to Do" page opposite it.

2. Turn the page to see our Rewrite. Read "What We Did" to improve the original.

You can also use this book as a reference any time you need help with a particular type of letter.

POSITION OF DATES AND SIGNATURES

Whether you choose to indent the date at the top of your letter and the signature at the bottom is a matter of personal or company style. Both the traditional forty-space indent and the contemporary flush-left format are equally correct. For simplicity, the flush-left style is used throughout this book.

CHAPTER 4

Agreements

You've talked, you think you've agreed, and now it's time to describe and confirm that agreement in a letter. Agreement letters are invaluable tools for confirming that an agreement actually exists and that it is what both parties think it is. An agreement letter can be an informal letter of understanding with no response required (unless the recipient disagrees). It can also be a more formal document that both parties sign, a sort of mini-contract.

Why bother, when you're already clear about who has agreed to do what? Because good-intentioned people sometimes misunderstand or forget. Seeing your version of the agreement in black and white helps you notice any inconsistencies or omissions and refine your thinking. It also helps the reader who may say, "Wait a minute—I thought *you* were going to do that!"

A clearly written letter of understanding or agreement can save time, money, and needless animosity. Turn the page and begin your first assignment.

MONUMENTAL IRRIGATION CORPORATION

February 3, 1995

Mr. Gerald Wildman
General Manager, Minnow Dam Project
Spector Corporation
117 Mountain Road
River City, WI 43251

RE: MINNOW DAM PROJECT
CONTRACTUAL CONSIDERATION—RIGHTS OF MIC
SA 1004523 ABD—329   FILE 04432—2

Dear Gerry:

Monumental Irrigation Corporation (MIC) has been made aware of certain problems (including but not limited to containment) relating to its Minnow Dam twin unit nuclear plant and the equipment and related services which Spector is supplying to that project. In order to facilitate the successful completion of construction and to avoid the need to institute litigation during the pendency of such construction, MIC hereby notifies Spector Corporation, its divisions, subsidiaries, affiliates and its and their agents, successors, employees and assign (''Spector'') and all other persons, parties, associations, firms or corporations which may be jointly or severally liable with any or all of those mentioned, that any past, present or future approvals, actions or payments of or by MIC relating to, directly or indirectly, in any manner whatsoever, the furnishing of equipment, the construction of any portion or part of or the provision of services in connection with the Minnow Dam Project, shall not be deemed and is not intended either expressly or impliedly, to constitute and is here expressly stated neither to have been nor to be a waiver or relinquishment of any and all past, present or future rights, claims, demands, actions, causes of action or suits at law in trespass (specifically including but not limited to negligence) or assumpsit, equity, or admiralty, whether known or unknown, or by contribution or indemnity, and without limitation of the foregoing, any and all other rights of MIC.

Very truly yours,

Gerald J. Alexanderson
Vice President
System Power Engineering

GJA: ed
Encl.

WHAT TO DO

This is a classic lawyer's letter, written to cover every possible contingency. It consists of two sentences, one of which contains 196 words!

Fortunately, the trend is to convert lawyer lingo to everyday language. If you *want* to be understood, you can be both clear and concise.

Imagine that you are a busy Spector employee. Can you find out in just a few seconds what you are being asked to do? Is your willingness to respond in inverse ratio to the length of time it takes to figure out what is wanted of you?

1. Underline any problem/s the writer mentions.

2. Circle what the writer says Monumental Irrigation Corporation is willing to do in spite of the problem/s.

3. Put a check next to the reason/s they are willing to do this.

WHAT WE DID

ANSWERS

1. Problems mentioned by writer:
   ". . . certain problems (including but not limited to containment relating to its Minnow Dam twin unit nuclear plant and the equipment and related services which Spector is supplying to that project."

2. After saying they don't want to hold up completion, Monumental describes "future payments," implying that they will continue paying.

3. They will continue paying
   "In order to facilitate the successful completion of construction and to avoid the need to institute litigation during the pendency of such construction, ..."

OUR REWRITE

The Rewrite was also written by a lawyer and covers the same contingencies, but it is much easier to read and understand.

We have added a request for the reader to sign and return a copy of the letter to show that he agrees to the conditions.

REWRITE

MONUMENTAL IRRIGATION CORPORATION

February 3, 1995

Mr. Gerald Wildman
General Manager, Minnow Dam Project
Spector Corporation
117 Mountain Road
River City, WI 43251

RE: MINNOW DAM PROJECT
CONTRACTUAL CONSIDERATION—RIGHTS OF MIC
SA 1004523 ABD—329   FILE 04432—2

Dear Gerry:

Despite the problems we've had with Spector on the Minnow Dam Project, we are going to continue to make payments to Spector in order not to delay construction any further.

MIC is not waiving its rights to assert claims against Spector with respect to any aspect of Spector's performance on the project.

Please indicate Spector's acceptance of this reservation by signing and returning the enclosed copy of this letter.

Very truly yours,

Gerald J. Alexanderson
Vice President
System Power and Engineering

Accepted and Agreed:
SPECTOR CORPORATION
BY:_____
Vice President

Encl: Duplicate letter

CITY OF SPECTORVILLE

October 1, 1994

Ms. Tammy Thrip, Group Coordinator
Holly Travel Group
Spectorville, CA 99999

Dear Tammy:

Our conversation on September 16, 1994, was very informative. The following items were discussed and will alleviate any confusion between the City of Spectorville and the Holly Travel Group. Please read the following items we discussed on September 16, 1994, and sign and return them to me at your earliest convenience. This letter will constitute agreements between the City of Spectorville and the Holly Travel Group for the 1994-1995 Winter Snow Ski Season.

A) The City of Spectorville will not incur any financial liability for unused seats if a Spectorville representative contacts a Holly Travel Group representative the Monday preceding departure (five working days in advance) for a one-day ski trip and two (2) Mondays preceding departure (ten working days in advance) for a weekend trip. (Note: Working days are considered Monday through Friday.)

B) All financial reservation deposits will be waived for the City of Spectorville.

C) Holly Travel Group will refund the City of Spectorville for all unused seats within two (2) weeks after the date of the trip.

D) Holly Travel Group transportation will pick up the City of Spectorville participants at the Joe Sharkey Recreational Center, 1120 Roosevelt Avenue in Spectorville if all seats reserved are occupied.

I have read and understand the information in this letter.

_____   _____
DAN C. O'DOUL   TAMMY THRIP
City of Spectorville   Holly Travel Group
Park and Recreation Dept.

WHAT TO DO

This writer has highlighted the points of the agreement with ABCs. He has provided a place for the reader to sign and return a copy of the letter if she agrees that it describes their conversation accurately. Let's make this letter better.

1. The best thing you can do for your reader is to put the purpose up front:

   - Underline the purpose of the letter. If you cannot find one, suggest one here:

   - Put a star next to each action the writer is asking the reader to take.

2. Does the writer give a time limit for responding?

3. Suggest a heading for each of the four points of the agreement.

4. Point A covers two different situations. How could you emphasize this to avoid confusion?

WHAT WE DID

ANSWERS

1. The *purpose* of the letter is implied: to summarize the agreement reached in a previous conversation. The *action* is requested in the final sentence: to sign and return the copy of the agreement.

2. No response date was indicated. It is important to give busy people a time frame for acting on your requests. We have added a reasonable deadline in the first sentence of the Rewrite.

3. Our suggested headings are in the Rewrite opposite.

4. The two subdivisions are:

   • For a one-day ski trip
   • For a weekend trip

We have highlighted these two options with bullets.

OUR REWRITE

The statement before the signature could be more explicit. We have moved a sentence from the first paragraph of the Original to introduce the signature in the Rewrite.

REWRITE

CITY OF SPECTORVILLE

October 1, 1994

Ms. Tammy Thrip, Group Coordinator
Holly Travel Group
Spectorville, CA 99999

Dear Tammy:

The letter outlines our discussion on September 16, 1994. If you agree, please sign and return the attached copy to me by October 10.

A) Penalty for Unused Seats. The City of Spectorville will not incur any financial liability for unused seats if a Spectorville representative contacts a Holly Travel Group representative:
   • For a one-day ski trip, the Monday preceding departure (five working days in advance).
   • For a weekend trip, two (2) Mondays preceding departure (ten working days in advance).
     Note: Working days are considered Monday through Friday.

B) Waiving of Deposits. All financial reservation deposits will be waived for the City of Spectorville.

C) Refund Schedule. Holly Travel Group will refund the City of Spectorville for all unused seats within two (2) weeks after the date of the trip.

D) Transportation. Holly Travel Group transportation will pick up the City of Spectorville participants at the Joe Sharkey Recreational Center, 1120 Roosevelt Avenue in Spectorville, if all reserved seats are occupied.

I agree that this letter constitutes the agreements between the City of Spectorville and Holly Travel Group for the 1994-1995 Winter Snow Ski Season.

_____   _____
DAN C. O'DOUL   TAMMY THRIP
City of Spectorville   Holly Travel Group
Park & Recreation Dept.

Encl: Copy of Agreement Letter

Your Perfect Letter Checklist

☑ **PUT YOUR PURPOSE UP FRONT**

Why are you writing? Let the reader know immediately in your first sentence or, if some background is *absolutely* essential, in your first paragraph.

If you are writing for several reasons, start your letter:

We need to straighten out three problems:

Follow this with headings for each subject so the reader can scan the page and know within seconds what you are writing about:

```
We need to straighten out three problems
before the January audit:
Missing Check: (followed by text)
Late Payment: (followed by text)
Overpayment: (followed by text)
```

CHAPTER 5

Announcements

Whether you're announcing a breakfast speech by your vice president at a Rotary Club or a major plant renovation that will disrupt traffic and parking for thousands of people, write what the readers may need to know. Then arrange that information so they can "get the news" immediately.

Use headings, spacing, and indentations to arrange the information so the main points can be grasped easily. Even if—*especially* if—your announcement comes under the category of "bad news," making people struggle to read and understand it won't help them take it any better.

THE COLLEGE CLARION   and   RADIO STATION WITS

INVITE YOU TO A PUBLICITY WORKSHOP

October 31, 1995
Dear Friends:

The College Clarion and WITS cordially invite you or a representative of
your organization, department, or living group to a publicity workshop on
Wednesday, November 8, from 4 to 6 P.M. in the Clarion Room.

We are both faced continually by questions of why we did not cover a
particular event. Quite often the answer is a lack of communications between
the sponsoring group and us.

We want to overcome this gap by exchanging ideas on how your organization can
best communicate with us. And a publicity workshop is the logical step
toward successfully reaching out to the college community.

The Clarion and WITS have complementary publicity services that can be
offered to your organization. At the workshop we will each offer a half-hour
presentation on our respective needs and services, including news policies,
deadlines, and effective ways of expressing your ideas. Before closing, the
workshop will be opened to feedback, questions, and suggestions.

We would hope that after attending this workshop you could return to your
organization with a better idea of how we operate, as well as the services we
can best offer each other.

This forum will be beneficial to the whole college campus. We all have the
same goal of reaching the whole community, and the better we work together,
the easier that goal becomes attainable. We look forward to seeing you on
November 8.

Sincerely,

STANLEY LAUREL   OLIVER N. HARDY
Editor   Station Manager
The College Clarion   WITS

WHAT TO DO

As a busy person, you know what it is like to get this kind of well-meaning but hard-to-grasp communication. Do you take the time to figure out what the writer wants? Or do you spend a few seconds, then set it aside for later (or drop it in the round filing cabinet)?

Two organizations dedicated to publicity—a radio station and a newspaper—should be able to produce an easy-to-read persuasive announcement. When they don't communicate clearly, you may suspect the quality of workshop they are sponsoring.

1. Underline the reason the writer is writing.
2. Play newspaper reporter and put a check next to each of the classic Five Ws of journalism in the original letter. Jot them down here.

Who:
What:
When:
Where:
Why:

WHAT WE DID

ANSWERS

1. The purpose is to announce a publicity workshop.
2. Who: the *College Clarion* and Radio Statio WITS
   What: the workshop
   When: Wednesday, November 8
   Where: Clarion Room
   Why: teach publicity skills that could benefit community

OUR REWRITE

The date, time, and place are nearly impossible to miss when they are highlighted by centering each on a separate line.

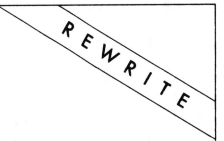

October 31, 1995

Dear Friends:

THE COLLEGE CLARION and RADIO STATION WITS

<u>INVITE YOU TO A PUBLICITY WORKSHOP</u>

Wednesday, November 8

4 to 6 P.M.

Clarion Room

- ''Why didn't our organization's story get printed?''
- ''What happened to our department announcement?''
- ''How can my living group's fund raiser get publicity?''

Tune in Wednesday, November 8, and learn how we all can work together to get your message across, to benefit everyone in our community. Discover how the complementary publicity services of the <u>Clarion</u> and WITS can work for you, what our deadlines are, how to reach us, and what to tell us.

Then give us your feedback, questions, and suggestions.

We look forward to seeing you there.

STANLEY LAUREL   OLIVER N. HARDY
Editor   Station Manager
<u>The College Clarion</u>   WITS

SPECTORVILLE ASSOCIATION

Welcome, and thank you for taking the time to serve on the Franchise Advisory Committee. We are looking forward to working with you this week. Hopefully you have had no trouble with plane or travel arrangements through Spector Travel. Please let us know if there have been or are any hitches.

We will be starting tomorrow morning with a continental breakfast at 8:30 in our meeting room for the week, Hospitality Room #417. The meeting will begin at 9:00.

Here at the Hotel Regency, the master billing for Spector includes your room, telephone, meals, and tax. The master bill will not, however, include any incidentals or personal items you might purchase in the hotel gift shop, for instance.

On Wednesday evening, July 13, we are hosting a dinner party in your honor. We will be dining at the Deer Trail Golf Club, with dinner starting at 8:30 after cocktails at 8:00. Some of you have rented cars, and car-pooling to the dinner will be arranged during the week.

For your other meals, there is a coffee shop in the hotel, the Terrace Cafe, and, on the top floor of the hotel, Tip Top. Tip Top is very popular locally, so we recommend that you make reservations a day in advance to be assured a place. Please keep your receipts for any expenses not included on the hotel bill and you will be reimbursed.

Again, welcome to Spectorville. We are looking forward to meeting with you on Monday morning and to working with you throughout the week. Please don't hesitate to call Gracie Fields at 874-3944, extension 106, if there is anything you need.

John Loder   Gracie Fields
Manager of Corporate and   Senior Training Coordinator
Retail Curriculum

WHAT TO DO

You arrive in a strange city for a conference, and this letter is waiting for you. How helpful would you find it? Let's make it even more useful.

1. Put a check next to every scheduled event. Make a time chart of them here:

2. What other topics are covered? Put a star next to each of them and write suggested headings.

WHAT WE DID

ANSWERS

1. The timetable of events appears in our Rewrite under the heading *"Highlights of Schedule."*
2. Three other topics in the letter are:

   Meals

   Expenses

   Travel Problems

   Information/Contact

   (Need Help? Have a Question?)

OUR REWRITE

We have created a timetable to which busy attendees can refer and have arranged the information under headings.

SPECTORVILLE ASSOCIATION

Dear Committee Members:

Welcome to Spectorville and thank you for taking the time to serve on the Franchise Advisory Committee. We are looking forward to working with you this week.

Highlights of Schedule

Monday, July 11	8:30 A.M.	Continental breakfast in Hospitality Room #417
	9:00 A.M.	Meeting begins, Room 417
Wednesday, July 13	8:00 P.M.	Cocktails at the Deer Trail Golf Club, prior to:
	8:30 P.M.	A dinner party in your honor. (Car-pooling will be arranged during the week.)

Meals: For your other meals, there is the Terrace Cafe coffee shop in the hotel, and also the Tip Top on the top floor. The Tip Top is very popular locally, so we recommend making reservations a day ahead. Be sure to save your receipts for reimbursement.

Expenses: The master billing for Spector at the Hotel Regency includes your room, telephone, meals, and tax. The master bill will not include any incidentals such as personal purchases at the gift shop. Please keep receipts for any reimbursable expenses not included in the hotel bill (such as meals) and turn them in to _____ (name) by _____ (date).

Travel Problems? If you have (or had) any hitches with travel arrangements made through Spector Travel, let us know.

Need Help? Have a Question? We are looking forward to meeting with you on Monday morning and to working with you throughout the week. Please don't hesitate to call Gracie Fields at 874-3944, extension 106, if there is anything you need.

John Loder
Manager of Corporate and
Retail Curriculum

Gracie Fields
Senior Training Coordinator

Your Perfect Letter Checklist

☑ **USE ACTIVE VERBS**

Sometimes we try so hard to be diplomatic that we don't say directly what we want done. We think that after we have laid out all the pertinent information, our reader will be clever enough to know intuitively what we really want to happen. Too often such diplomacy only leads to frustration and waste. This is especially true in Instruction Letters.

The English language has two kinds of verbs: transitive (direct, acting on something) and intransitive (indirect, passive.) Use *direct* verbs whenever possible.

(thumbs up) SAY:	(thumbs down) NOT:
Will you call them immediately to ask for a refund?	They ought to be contacted about a refund.
Please pay your account quarterly starting next month.	Our new policy, pursuant to clause 1-04387, requires quarterly payments on type EC-47 and ED-47 accounts.
Mail your overseas fourth-class Christmas packages by November 15th.	Fourth-class shipments require five weeks to reach overseas destinations.
Please fill out these forms and return them to me by June 1st.	Forms should be processed in a timely manner.

CHAPTER 6

Angry Letters

Angry words are a power tool. Like a chain saw, they can get a lot done when used properly. And, like a chain saw, they can also do a lot of damage when they run wild.

There are many situations where anger is more than justified. We are never more brilliant or more devastating than when we write in the heat of righteous anger. That's why the two-step Perfect Letter technique is invaluable for angry letters.

EXPLORATORY PHASE

Say how furious you are. Identify the guilty and describe their conduct. List all the reasons why you are angry. Use any language you wish.

CRAFTING PHASE

Start by making a statement about what you want to be different after the reader reads this letter. *Of course* you want the reader to know that you are angry, but is that your only goal? You probably have another. If your first goal is fairly unobtainable (like "world peace" or "less stupidity"), write a second-choice goal, being as specific as possible: "two-week turn around" or "rectify error within twenty-four hours." Then evaluate your list of reasons and your goal statement to decide what this particular reader needs to know to bring about your desire.

Ask yourself, "Is my anger directed at the right target? Can that target handle my anger—that is, will s/he be more or less willing and able to carry out my wishes after reading these words?" Use your power tool wisely for maximum productivity.

ORIGINAL

SPECTOR MOTOR CORPORATION

March 4, 1998

Mr. F. X. Bushman
Customer Service Manager
Spector Motor Corporation
BY MESSENGER

Letter of Warning

Dear Frank:

This morning I visited your office and found Alyssa at her desk and Charlene
not at her desk. A few minutes later the phones began to ring and I looked up
to find both secretarial desks vacated. Alyssa was in the copy room. One of
two reasons for this unacceptable situation must be applicable. Either you
have not explained the priority of the telephones to your secretaries or
your secretaries have chosen to ignore the instructions.

In an economic environment as difficult as we have now, we cannot afford to
ignore ringing phones. We have eliminated jobs because of lack of orders and
we have spent significant money to alter our office area to make us more
responsive. I will not tolerate any lack of buy-in on anyone's part to our
objective of improved customer response which starts with answering phones.
I will not even tolerate inadequate phone coverage for the rest of today.
Consequently, I require the following actions to occur by the team meeting
tomorrow morning.

First, the telehone answering requirements are to be transmitted in writing
to both secretaries with copies to me and to Louise Glaum.

Second, an arrangement must be made with an agency to cover us quickly when
either secretary is out sick.

Louise Glaum has convinced me that I should not handle this situation
directly, so you must resolve this problem immediately.

Starting next week, leaving the phones unattended during work hours without
approval of the operations manager must result in immediate disciplinary
action in exact accordance with company policies: verbal warning for first
offense, written warning for the second, probation for the third, and
immediate termination for the fourth.

Sincerely,

Lupino Lane
Division Manager

WHAT TO DO

Angry letters usually make the writer feel good and the readers feel rotten. To be useful, an angry letter should result in corrective action. If the writer blows off steam first, the readers may be so overwhelmed that they miss the instructions, so angry that they stop understanding, or so devastated that they have little motive to carry them out.

Letters of warning are one of the most common types of angry letters. Let's assume that this Original letter was *not* written in response to a long series of infractions, that this is the first time the problem has been observed. The anger comes from frustration that an essential company survival policy is not being carried out.

Reword this letter so that it becomes a problem-solving letter that results in action, not panic or resentment.

1. Put the purpose up front in an opening sentence. Jot it here:

2. List the things the reader is being asked to do in the order he is being asked to do them.

3. Draw a line under other information that the reader needs to know to achieve the writer's purpose.

WHAT WE DID

ANSWERS

1. Purpose up front: The opening sentence has been changed from

   "This morning I visited your office and found Alyssa at her desk and Charlene not at her desk."

   to

   "There is an urgent problem in your department that needs your immediate attention: some incoming calls are not being answered."

2. The things the reader is being asked to do are in the Rewrite under "What I want you to do."

3. The reader needs to know

   - the urgency of answering phones
   - background on why
   - background on the specific incident that prompted the letter.

4. The reader probably doesn't need to know

   - the details of possible future disciplinary action at this point—presumably it hasn't been established yet that this problem cannot be remedied by Mr. Bushman's intervention or that he is unwilling or unable to correct it.
   - that Louise Glaum asked Mr. Lane not to speak directly to the secretaries.

OUR REWRITE

We've changed the headline "Letter of Warning" (an official step toward dismissal) to the more action-promoting, less-threatening "Urgent Warning."

We've framed the letter so that it asks for and expects the expertise of the reader to solve the problem, offering any support that he may need to do so.

SPECTOR MOTOR CORPORATION

March 4, 1998

Mr. F. X. Bushman
Customer Service Manager
Spector Motor Corporation
BY MESSENGER

Re: <u>Urgent Warning</u>

Dear Frank:

There is an urgent problem in your department that needs your immediate attention: some incoming calls are not being answered.

I need your immediate action <u>today</u> to solve any contributing problems and to insure that this will never happen again. I am counting on you to reemphasize our policy of covering the telephones at all times <u>no matter what</u> to the people in your department and to authorize them to refuse any demand for their services from anyone in the company—myself included—if it means that the telephones won't be covered for even a moment.

This is both policy and our top priority! You know that we have eliminated jobs because of lack of orders and have spent significant money to make our office area more responsive.

<u>Background</u>: When I visited your office this morning, **Alyssa was at her** desk, Charlene was not. A few minutes later the phones **began to ring and I** looked up to find both secretarial desks vacant. Alyssa **was in the copy room.**

<u>What I want you to do</u>:

1. Make absolutely sure the phones are covered for the rest of today!
2. Counsel both secretaries in person and in writing. Send copies of your instructions to me and Louise Glaum.
3. Make an advance arrangement with a personnel agency for immediate coverage when either secretary is out sick.
4. Be ready to report at the team meeting tomorrow morning on what steps you have taken and what help you may need to see that this <u>never</u> happens again.

I'm confident you can resolve this so that official disciplinary warnings won't be necessary. We'll talk more tomorrow.

Sincerely,

Lupino Lane
Division Manager

WHAT ABOUT A REAL DISMISSAL THREAT?

Now suppose that this problem has happened before and that this letter is the official second-warning letter mentioned in the last paragraph of the Original.

The alternate Rewrite on the opposite page has been crafted to be a formal reprimand, one of the steps in an official termination process. Note that it still offers to help the reader solve the problem before it lists possible punishments.

SPECTOR MOTOR CORPORATION

March 4, 1998

Mr. F. X. Bushman
Customer Service Manager
Spector Motor Corporation
BY MESSENGER

Re: <u>Letter of Warning</u>

Dear Frank:

I need your immediate action <u>today</u> to prevent any more recurrences of the problem I observed this morning when I visited your department: as during my February visit, telephones went unanswered because both secretaries were away from their desks. We discussed then how this violates Spector policy, especially with the recent layoffs due to lack of sales and the extra investment to prevent just this thing happening.

<u>Background</u>:   At 9:15 A.M. today Alyssa was at her desk, Charlene was not. A few minutes later both desks were vacant and the phones began to ring. Alyssa was in the copy room.

<u>What I want you to do</u>:

   1.   Make absolutely sure the phones are covered every minute for the rest of today!
   2.   Counsel both secretaries in person and in writing. Send copies of your instructions to me and Louise Glaum.
   3.   Make an advance arrangement with a personnel agency for immediate coverage when either secretary is out sick.
   4.   Be ready to report at the team meeting tomorrow morning on what steps you have taken and what help you may need to see that this <u>never</u> happens again.

<u>Your Official Warning</u>: You have already had an official verbal warning. This constitutes official written warning in accordance with company policy. If the phones are again left unattended during work hours without approval of the operations manager, the next two steps, as you know, will be probation for a third warning and immediate termination following a fourth warning.

But I'm sure we can lick this before it comes to that. Let's solve this problem together now!

Sincerely,

Lupino Lane
Division Manager

SPECTORVILLE NURSERY

June 11, 1995

Mr. Roger Hapless
Spectorville Nursery

Letter of Warning

Dear Roger Hapless:

The blatant, insubordinate, and emotional outbursts such as you demonstrated this past Wednesday evening and Thursday morning will not be tolerated. In my opinion, your actions were totally without provocation. Just for the record, I would like to be more specific with regards to the incident in question.

On Wednesday, June 8, 1995:

1. Overpowering Tool Room man with verbal abuse to the point of fear of violence.
2. Taking tools without permission, known to be in direct violation of the rules.
3. Failure to return tools.
4. Request by Bob Jones to return tools was defiantly ignored.
5. Response to further request to comply resulted in reckless driving, skidding of tires, and throwing of keys at Tool Room cage.
6. Because of your overt hostility, I elected not to pursue the matter further; instead I chose to continue the discussion the following morning.
7. To account for and adequately secure the remainder of the tools for the night, I had the Tool Room man remove them from your truck.

On Thursday, June 9, 1995:

8. At the staff meeting Thursday morning regarding tools, you were defiant and hostile—embarrassment to your men and to me as well.
9. After the meeting, you went to the Tool Room once again, becoming irrational. I asked you to calm down and obey the rules or leave the premises.

It is my belief you should seek professional help in dealing with serious personal problems, which are causing obvious pressure and tension, prompting these recurring displays of anger and generally erratic behavior.

During previous conversations, I have offered the confidential resources of our Personnel Department, which would assist you in finding help. It is imperative that I know what steps you plan to take, Roger, to rectify this very serious situation.

Mike de Angeles, Manager

WHAT TO DO

There are few things more frightening than being confronted by a person out of control. This writer is oviously both furious and afraid. He has a right to be both. Now it is time for him to craft his letter to achieve its purpose: to change the way Roger Hapless behaves or to dismiss him. Considering the frequent newspaper accounts of disgruntled employees who come gunning for supervisors, it can be both good business practice and a practical personal safety measure to change the focus of a letter of warning from punishment of the employee to joint problem-solving directed at the offending behavior.

This writer is making a request and a suggestion, both of which could be lost in the emotions of the situation.

1. Put a check next to the offer of help. Which paragraph is it in? Is the reader likely to see it before he reacts violently, throwing the letter away or ripping it up?

2. Circle the writer's recommendation to the reader. Where should that recommendation go?

3. The writer has numbered items, believing that he is creating a list. Unfortunately not all items in his list are equal. Put a star next to those items that describe what Roger did. Start each with a statement: "You. . . ."

4. How could you increase white space to make the points stand out?

5. Do you know the procedure in your organization for a letter of reprimand such as this? Who must approve? Who must receive copies? How do these constraints affect your writing a letter of reprimand?

WHAT WE DID

ANSWERS

1. The purpose is to force Roger Hapless to take steps to change the situation. We put this first, before we started berating him about his offenses.

2. The writer's recommendation is in the last two paragraphs. Again, before listing the offenses and stirring hostile memories, we put the recommendation of professional, confidential services up front.

3. We isolated Wednesday's action as:

   - "You abused . . ."
   - "You took . . ."
   - "You failed . . ."
   - "You ignored . . ."
   - "You drove . . ."

   We identified the Thursday actions as:

   - "You were . . ."
   - "You went . . ."

4. We used indents and underlines to make the page (if not the message) more appealing.

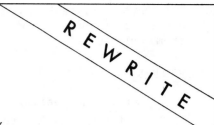

SPECTORVILLE NURSERY

June 11, 1995

Mr. Roger Hapless
Spectorville Nursery

<u>Letter of Warning</u>

Dear Roger:

You are obviously under a lot of pressure. I need to know immediately what steps you plan to take to rectify the very serious situation that has developed because of your recurring displays of anger and erratic behavior.

During our previous conversations I have offered the confidential services of our Personnel Department to assist you in finding professional help. That offer still goes.

Roger, I'm sure you realize that any future insubordination and incidents like what happened this past Wednesday and Thursday will result in your immediate dismissal. You must decide now what you want to do.

For the record, here is what I believe happened:

<u>On Wednesday, June 8, 1995</u>

1. You verbally abused the Tool Room supervisor so that he feared violence.
2. You took tools without permission, which you know is a direct violation of the rules.
3. You then failed to return the tools to Bob Jones.
4. You defiantly ignored my request to return the tools.
5. When you were again asked to comply, you went to your truck, drove it recklessly around the parking lot, skidded noisily to a stop at the loading door, and then threw the car keys at the Tool Room cage.

Because of your emotional state, I didn't pursue the matter until we could discuss it the next morning. I had the Tool Room supervisor remove the tools from your truck.

On Thursday, June 9, 1995

1. At a staff meeting on the problem, you were defiant and hostile.
2. After the meeting you went to the Tool Room and once again acted in an irrational manner. I asked you to calm down and obey the rules or leave the premises.

Your actions this past Wednesday evening and Thursday morning seemed totally without provocation. You will understand that I cannot tolerate any future outbursts. They are very distressing to all your coworkers and disrupt the entire plant. How can I help?

Sincerely,

Mike de Angeles, Manager

CHAPTER 7

Apologies

Don't be afraid to say "I'm sorry."

Some executives have a phobia against using the expression in a business letter. Perhaps it's because they believe a company can't be sorry. But companies consist of and are run by people. The more companies act that way, the better the people who deal with them like it.

When you or your company have made a mistake or let someone down, don't hesitate to apologize, even if (*especially* if) it's not your fault.

If you're wrong, say so immediately. Here are opening paragraphs taken from two excellent letters of apology.

- "If it weren't illegal, Mr. Curtis, I'd enclose my head with this letter. We have taken far too long to reply to your June 7 requisition, No. 402."

- "The delay on your shipment, P.O. 29976, is entirely my fault. I goofed when I entered your order and did not specify that it should be sent to your Milwaukee office. To try to make up for this, I am . . ."

SPECTOR CORPORATION

July 12, 1994

Mrs. Harrold Lear
4725 Nickol Street
Chicago, IL 60611

Dear Mrs. Lear:

First of all, Mrs. Lear, we are truly and genuinely disturbed to learn from your recent letter that you are unhappy about the service you recently received from our Parts Department.

The statement in our June 15 letter that the Order Pads were sent to you on June 4 was entirely truthful. Without indulging in self-praise, we do make a sincere and honest attempt to ship orders promptly, but we have little or no control over shipments after they leave our place of business. Of that I am sure you understand, Mrs. Lear.

Looking at this situation from your point of view, we can see why you have cause to be critical of our service. Perhaps you would in the future prefer to send your orders to our Detroit office. Our Denver office is set up, as I feel sure you can understand, to expedite shipments to our valued customers in the Middle West. However, as I previously explained to you, you were caught between our two offices, for which I am deeply and truly sorry.

But let's continue on a more positive note. Immediately upon receipt of your valued letter this morning, I personally went to the Warehouse and pulled the enclosed Order Pads. Enclosed are two each of those Pads which you requested.

We value you both as a customer and as a friend, Mrs. Lear, and we will do everything that is in our power to keep our relationship on a friendly basis. Won't you please write us and let us know, at your very earliest convenience, if everything is entirely satisfactory now, please?

With sincere regrets,

Mrs. Roberta Fowler

WHAT TO DO

This fulsome apology is obviously a response to an angry customer. The apologies are so profuse, they may end up sounding insincere despite the good intentions of the writer.

The recipient probably wants only two things:

- some sympathy—validation of her anger
- a solution

You can give her these two things briefly and effectively in your Rewrite.

However, you may also be tempted to speculate on how the shipment got lost—that is, to give an excuse. Usually, such explanations smack of "It's someone else's fault" and should be offered only if the information can help the reader prevent future problems. (Does he or she really care whose fault it is?) And of course, if you really goofed, admit it without elaborate justifications.

Remember, the customer will be more influenced by what you are *doing* to correct the mistake and solve the problem than by what you are *saying* in your own defense.

1. Rewriting the opening sentence is a matter of tone. If you talk like that in person, leave it as written. If you are less effusive, try writing a new opening sentence of apology that sounds just as sincere.

2. Tell how you are solving the customer's problem. (Make up any details that are not in the original letter.)

3. Figure out how to convey the information about ordering from the Detroit office in the future without making it sound like a criticism of the reader's past conduct.

4. Add any appropriate citations for enclosures, subject, etc.

WHAT WE DID

ANSWERS

1. The Rewrite's opening sentence combines an apology and a statement of the problem.

2. The Rewrite includes details about how the problem is being solved rather than guesses about what may have happened. We have dropped the request that the customer take the time to write a reply stating whether the new shipment was received and if everything is now satisfactory. (If you were already peeved, would such a request for your time make you feel better?) Instead we've stated that the writer will telephone to be sure the new shipment has arrived. This demonstrates her concern for satisfying the customer and her tenacity in following up any problem the customer may have. It also saves the customer a lot of time. This businesslike "service" approach can do more to ensure customer loyalty than begging to be allowed "to keep the relationship on a friendly basis" in the future.

3. Informing the customer that she really should have ordered from another office is difficult in the context of an apology letter. Perhaps this information should be sent after the problem has been solved. If it is absolutely necessary to include it in this letter, we suggest adding it as a post script so that it doesn't seem to be a criticism of the reader or related to her problem.

4. The original order is cited under the address. The enclosures are listed at the bottom.

SPECTOR CORPORATION

July 12, 1994

Mrs. Harrold Lear
4725 Nickol Street
Chicago, IL 60611

Your order P.O. 12345, May 1, 1994

Dear Mrs. Lear:

We are tremendously sorry to hear that the order pads we shipped you on June 4 have never arrived. I have made up a duplicate of your original shipment for you and am enclosing two each of the different styles you requested. The rest of your pads will go out to you this afternoon by regular freight and should reach you within ten days.

I apologize for the inconvenience this has caused you and will do everything I can to find out what happened so we can prevent such delays in the future. I'll call you in a few days to confirm that these pads have arrived.

Sincerely,

Mrs. Roberta Fowler

Encl: 8 order pads: 2 ea. #123, #234, #345, #456

P.S. Shipping time to Chicago is only five days from our Detroit office. You may prefer ordering through them in the future. Their address is:

SPECTOR CORPORATION
2199 West Street
Detroit, MI 44444
tel: 1-333-487-9999.

SPECTOR, INC.

February 18, 1999

Mr. Charles Wolfe
1702 East Drive
River Falls, WI 61111

Dear Mr. Wolfe:

We are writing in response to your January 18, 1999, letter concerning your account with Beecher-Waterfield, Inc. for whom we at Spector act as Clearing Agent.

By way of explanation, Mr. Wolfe, the sum of $187.68 in your account represents a debit balance. Enclosed are copies of various monthly statements, as well as the Standard and Poor's Stock Dividend Record for 1998, showing that your sale of 238 shares of Trans-America Communications common stock settled on June 17, 1998. Since this was after the Record Date of June 15, 1998, you were entitled to the July 15, 1998, dividend for $161.84, which was duly credited at that date. A check for this amount was issued on August 12, 1998.

However, because of delays in the transfer process, the certificates we received from you on June 11, 1998, were registered in your name on the Record Date of June 15, 1998. Therefore, you should have received another payment for $161.84 for the July 15, 1998, dividend directly from the Transfer Agent.

To reflect your receipt of duplicate dividend payments on your 238 shares of Trans-America Communications, we debited you for $161.84 on November 2, 1998. We are in the process of reversing our November 25, 1998, entry which erroneously debited you for $25.84, which will place your account at its proper debit balance of $161.84.

If you would kindly send a check for $161.84 to the attention of the undersigned at the above address, we will be glad to place your account in its proper zero balance.

Please accept our apologies for any inconveniences we may have caused and we hope the information provided will lead to an amicable and satisfactory resolution of this matter.

Sincerely yours,

Customer Service Manager
Agency Clearing Dept.

WHAT TO DO

Here is an actual letter received by a frustrated customer. Let's imagine that the customer is not a sophisticated financial expert but someone who may be easily confused by financial matters. Do you think the writer cleared up his problem or compounded it?

1. Describe Mr. Wolfe's problem briefly:

2. Describe the writer's explanation briefly:

3. What does the writer ask Mr. Wolfe to do to clear up the problem?

4. Is the tone of the letter conciliatory? If you were Mr. Wolfe, would you respond favorably to the explanation and request in this letter?

5. Craft an opening sentence that offers an apology, thanks the customer for pointing out the error, or in some way acknowledges that the customer is right.

6. Group background and supporting information together following the main points of a letter.

7. Include the name of the writer as well as the title, so the reader has a real person to contact.

8. List the enclosures at the bottom of the letter.

WHAT WE DID

ANSWERS

1. Mr. Wolfe's problem is that Spector has sent him a statement showing that he owes them $187.68, but he doesn't know why.

2. The writer says that $161.84 was debited against Mr. Wolfe's account because he was accidentally sent duplicate July dividend payments for that amount by Beecher-Waterfield and the Transfer Agent; $25.84 was deducted through another unspecific error.

3. The writer asks Mr. Wolfe to send him a check for $161.84. The request for repayment has been moved from paragraph five to paragraph two, immediately following an apology and a synopsis of the error.

4. Probably not—to both counts. Since the writer's company made the errors, Mr. Wolfe certainly deserves an apology, especially after waiting a month for reply to his inquiry letter. Tone is very important here. This is one case where the "vinegar" of honest contrition and plain facts may catch more flies than the "honey" of complex excuses and phrases like "an amicable and satisfactory conclusion to this matter." Amicable and satisfactory for whom? Spector caused Mr. Wolfe considerable trouble and now wants him to return money which they erroneously paid him.

5. See our Rewrite. Thanking the customer for complaining is quite honest. Customers who complain remain customers—those who don't complain go elsewhere.

6. We used an explanatory heading of "History of Error."

7. We had to create a name in this case, but customers generally prefer to have a name to contact if necessary.

8. Enclosures are grouped under the signature for the customer's convenience.

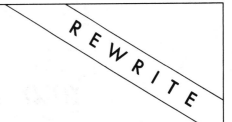

SPECTOR, INC.

February 18, 1999

Mr. Charles Wolfe
1702 East Drive
River Falls, WI 61111

Re: Your letter, January 18, 1999

Dear Mr. Wolfe:

Thank you for calling our attention to our errors on your account. We apologize for any inconvenience they may have caused you.

Current Status

Our errors were:
  • sending duplicate payments of $161.84
  • erroneously debiting your account for $25.84

When you send us a check for the $161.84 duplicate payment we made you, your account will again have a zero balance. You may send it to us at Spector as Clearing Agents for Beecher–Waterfield, Attn: Jeremy Elliott.

History of Error

Last June you sold 238 shares of Trans–American Communications common stock. Because of delays in the transfer process, you received a July dividend of $161.84 from us on August 12.

When we learned that the Transfer Agent should also have sent you a July dividend, we debited your account for the $161.84 on November 2.

Then on November 25, we erroneously debited your account for $25.84, producing the $187.68 debit figure ($161.84 + $25.85) on your statement. We have reversed that incorrect $25.84 charge.

I deeply regret any inconvenience our errors have caused you and hope that we will serve you better in the future.

Sincerely,

Jeremy Elliott
Customer Service Manager
Agency Clearing Department (999) 555–3333

Encl: Your monthly statements for June through November 1998
      Standard and Poor's Stock Dividend Record for 1998

Your Perfect Letter Checklist

☑ **USE SHORT PARAGRAPHS AND SENTENCES**

Is your writing easy to read?

When you talk, the tone of your voice, your pauses and inflections, can mean as much as your words. You provide natural separations to display your ideas.

When you write, the visual appeal of the page can encourage your reader to read on, pulling his eye from point to point. Or it can sabotage you entirely.

If you don't type your own correspondence, you may feel that this is something "the secretary should take care of." Of course, having a brilliant editor and layout artist who also types is helpful, but good format starts with good organization, and that starts with you.

CHAPTER 8

Asking for Action

When you want someone to do something, make it clear in your opening sentence. Often the impulse is to describe a situation in detail and then to put your request at the end. This traditional storytelling approach may seem the best way to justify your request, but it is unkind to your readers. They are not sure why they are reading and may bog down halfway through the page, entirely missing the real purpose of your letter.

Take the bottom line of your Exploratory Phase and put it first. Tell the reader what you want in the first paragraph or in a headline ("Re: _____"), then go on to offer background information, reasons, justifications, proofs, etc.

ORIGINAL

SPECTOR CORPORATION

September 13, 1999

Ross, Francis and Jeremy
Attorneys at Law
233 East Avenue
Detroit, MI 40050

Att: Mr. Peter A. Ross

Re: Michigan Questionnaire

Dear Mr. Ross:

Reference is made to our letter of July 9, 1999, wherein we indicated that we would be forwarding to you for review our answers to the Michigan Department of Revenue's questionnaire regarding our business activities in the state of Michigan.

Enclosed herewith please find a copy of our proposed answers and a copy of the questionnaire issued by the Michigan Department of Revenue.

We had originally thought we could submit these answers to you for review much earlier; however, events have not allowed us to do so and we would very much appreciate your prompt review and comments on this matter.

It is particularly important that you review these answers at your earliest convenience in light of the fact that we have communicated with the Michigan Department of Revenue indicating the answers would be in their office by September 10, 1999. While this date is not absolute, it does not look very good for us to get them the answers later than that date.

If you would be so kind as to write to the Michigan Department of Revenue advising them that you are reviewing our answers (at our request) and will be forwarding them on to the Department of Revenue upon completion, we would be most appreciative.

If you have any questions or comments, please feel free to call us.

Sincerely,

Paul James
Tax Administrator

Encl.

WHAT TO DO

Quick, what does the writer of this letter want? Does the subject "Michigan Questionnaire" help?

1. Circle what the writer is asking the reader to do.
2. Underline any sentences that explain why.
3. Cross out any information that is unnecessary.
4. Put a star next to the "zinger"—the astonishing information that tries to slip by in all the verbage.
5. What two important things are missing from this letter?

WHAT WE DID

ANSWERS

1. The reader is being asked to:

   - write to the Department of Revenue (paragraph 5)

   - review these answers at his earliest convenience (paragraph 4)

2. The sentence that explains why is the first sentence of paragraph 4.

3. Unnecessary information is found in most of paragraph one, all of paragraph two, the second half of paragraph three, most of paragraph four.

4. The "zinger" is in paragraph four: the questionnaire was due three days before this letter was written.

5. Two important things missing from this letter are:

   - a phone number or extension where the writer can be reached with questions

   - a list of enclosures

OUR REWRITE

We have changed the subject of the letter from:

"Re: Michigan Questionnaire"

to:

"Re: Your response to Michigan Questionnaire"

SPECTOR CORPORATION

September 13, 1999

Mr. Peter A. Ross
Ross, Francis and Jeremy
Attorneys at Law
233 East Avenue
Detroit, MI 40050

Re: Your Response to Michigan Questionnaire

Dear Mr. Ross:

The enclosed questionnaire is overdue because of a delay on our end. I'd be tremendously grateful if you could:

1. Write immediately to:
   Michigan Department of Revenue
   2896 Flint Avenue
   Royal Oaks, MI 48832

   advising them that you are reviewing our answers to their questions.
2. Review our proposed answers (enclosed) by September 20 and forward them to the Department of Revenue as soon as you are finished.

We promised them a reply by September 10, 1999, but obviously we were delayed. We are very sorry not to give you more time.

Sincerely,

Paul James
Tax Administrator (1-999-555-1111)

Encl: Michigan Questionnaire
     Our proposed answers

Ref: Our July 9, 1999, letter

CITY OF SPECTORVILLE

June 18, 1995

Mr. Evan Sledder
Spectorville Homeowners' Association
P.O. Box 9781
Spectorville, CA 97802

Dear Mr. Sledder:

On Monday, June 1, 1995, it was observed by our crew that the fence to the Recreation Club pool was in need of repair. We contacted you by telephone on June 11 and again on June 15, 1995, regarding this matter.

You stated in our phone conversations that you would temporarily fix the fence by using a padlock to hold the fence together. As discussed in our telephone conversation of June 15, it is our opinion that the fence should be fixed as soon as possible. As I explained, the two support posts were pulled out of the ground and kids could gain access by pulling or pushing it over.

I observed on Monday, June 18, 1995, that you have padlocked the fence together. We thank you for your cooperation, however, we feel this could still create a hazard to smaller children visiting the club area.

We hope that you agree and will fix the fence as soon as possible to its original condition.

You may contact me at (415) 555-9999 if you have further questions.

Sincerely,

Gail Thompson
Maintenance Supervisor

cc: Dorothy Lang, Standards Chair

WHAT TO DO

Here is a classic, both a once-upon-a-time letter and a CYA (cover your exposed rear flank) letter. The writer describes a potentially dangerous problem and then asks—in the *fourth* paragraph—for a solution. The letter carefully chronicles what has happened in case there are future questions or (tragically) a lawsuit.

This CYA letter is a valuable documentation of a serious situation. (Too often CYA letters are whiny in tone, crafted only to stress "It wasn't my fault!")

The writer of this letter (and it is real!) must have had good reasons for not accepting responsibility or ordering repairs. She says, "We hope you agree and will fix the fence," which seems an astonishingly docile way to approach such a potentially lethal problem. Apparently she doesn't have the authority to say "DO IT!" and is trying to be persuasive.

As you craft this letter, assume that the writer is very concerned about the problem, but not ready to appeal to a higher authority who might be able to demand action.

1. Underline the purpose of the letter. Write an opening sentence that expresses this purpose.

2. Can you think of a way to strengthen the persuasion? (Note that a heartfelt zinger like "Children are going to die!" could backfire, both legally and politically.) Hint: If the problem is urgent, should the writer say she will wait for the reader to call?

3. After answering question 2, do you want to change your opening sentence?

WHAT WE DID

ANSWERS

1. The purpose of the letter is in paragraph four of the Original:

   ```
   We hope that you agree and will fix the fence as
   soon as possible to its original condition.
   ```

   To strengthen this and make it a more direct request for action, we have added that the writer will telephone the reader on a specific date to learn the repair schedule.

2. No, the writer should probably not say she will wait for the reader to call if this is a request for action.

OUR REWRITE

Notice the dates of several past events that appear in the Original. Since the tone of this letter is still meant to signal the reader that his immediate cooperation is expected, we have not pulled them out under a formal heading. However, when and if the writer decides that friendly persuasion is unlikely to produce results and firmer methods are needed, she could make it clear that she is chronicling the events in case of future legal action or investigation:

History of Problem

June 1, 1995: Our crew filed a report that the fence of the Spectorville South Pool needed repair. Two support posts were pulled out of the ground and kids could gain access by pulling or pushing the fence over.

June 11: Dorothy Lang of our office called you to express our concern and to discuss your responsibility for repairs.

June 15: I called you and you said that you would make temporary repairs by using padlocks to hold the fence together.

June 18: I visited the site and was very pleased to see that you had made these temporary repairs.

It is hoped that the writer also keeps a telephone diary so that the history of the back and forth on this problem could be reconstructed later.

CITY OF SPECTORVILLE

June 18, 1995

Mr. Evan Sledder
Homeowners' Association
P.O. Box 9781
Spectorville, CA 97802

Repairs to Recreation Club Pool Fence

Dear Mr. Sledder:

I will call you Thursday morning to find out when you will be able to complete a permanent repair of the fence at the Recreation Club Pool. This problem was first observed by our crew more than three weeks ago on June 1, and should be fixed as soon as possible—or _sooner_—to eliminate the potential hazard for smaller children visiting the park, especially now that ''pool season'' is beginning.

In the meantime, thanks for your cooperation in making the temporary repair you suggested during our phone conversation on June 15: padlocking the fence together. I visited the site today and was very relieved to see this had been done.

However, as we discussed on June 11 after our crew noticed the problem and again on June 15, the two support posts have been pulled out of the ground and children could gain access by pulling or pushing the fence over.

Call me in the meantime at (1-415) 555-9999 if you have any questions or good news.

Sincerely,

Gail Thompson
Maintenance Supervisor

cc: Dorothy Lang, Standards Chair

SPECTOR, SPECTOR & SPECTOR

April 26, 1995

Mrs. Julia Garcia
15 Wedgewood Place
Cow Hollow, NY 10567

Re: Trial

Dear Julia:

As you know, the trial is presently set for May 23, 1995. I want to get together with you before that time and would appreciate your calling me about a week before the trial so that we can sit down and go over the facts again.

In the meantime, I want to prepare a financial statement to provide the court at the time of trial. I need to have a realistic appraisal of the real property at 15 Wedgewood Place. Would you communicate with some real estate broker in the area who is familiar with property in your area and who could give us the sale price of comparable residences in the last six months. With respect to the household furniture and furnishings, unless you and Mr. Garcia can agree as to the value and division, we must produce a list of all of the furniture and furnishings showing the purchase price, the year of acquisition, and your estimate of its present value. I am not talking about every nut and bolt, but about furniture and furnishings, appliances, silver, dishes, crystal, etc. I will also need a figure from you as to the value of the Chevrolet and Edsel. If there is any other property that you know of of any value, you should tell me about it so I can include it in my trial brief for the court's consideration. If there are any sums due on any of the property, I'd like to know what the balance was as of September 5, 1992, and what the balance due is as of May 1, 1995, or as close to that date as possible. Also, I notice in Mr. Garcia's response that he lists a 1992 Cadillac convertible, purchased by him after date of separation. If you have any information as to the source of the funds for the purchase of that car, I would appreciate your informing me.

In the financial declaration filed by Mr. Garcia, he indicates that you and he agreed privately that the First National Bank of Happy Valley auto loan, in the amount of $6,563, relating to the '78 Bentley, would be assumed by you in consideration of your obtaining ownership of the automobile and subject to an acknowledged equity of $2,000 in that automobile owed to Mr. Garcia. Additionally, they state that you each agreed to assume responsibility for one-half of an obligation in the amount of $3,100 owed to Charles Ramirez. I would like to discuss both of these matters with you when we meet.

You indicated to me when we met in November that $5,700 of your retirement fund went to repair flood damage. I would appreciate your looking for the bills and whatever substantiating evidence you have for this transaction and providing them to me for the trial.

Yours very truly,

JOHN L. SPECTOR
Attorney at Law

WHAT TO DO

Time is money.

This lawyer is probably keenly aware of the value of his time and may feel it isn't worth taking the few extra minutes to clarify his writing for the convenience of the reader. He has tried to think of everything he needs to learn from Julia Garcia before the trial. He probably dictated his thoughts into a dictaphone as he drove to work and had his secretary transcribe his stream-of-consciousness list.

However, if Mrs. Garcia arrives poorly prepared (or worse, fails to make the appointment, requiring a follow-up call), the lawyer has not saved his own time and may jeopardize his client's case.

What is the usual state of mind of anyone facing a trial? Will she easily pull out the list of everything she is being asked to do? What are the chances that she will make the appointment he requests and show up with all the data?

1. Put a check next to each thing the writer wants Julia Garcia to do.
2. Suggest a way to divide the information you have checked into categories.

3. Underline the requested response date.
4. Suggest a more informative RE: heading.

WHAT WE DID

ANSWERS

1. The things the writer wants Julia Garcia to do are enumerated in our Rewrite.

2. A natural division of these requests is:

3. The requested response date is unclear. She is to make an appointment for a meeting "about a week before the trial" on May 23. We have suggested May 5 as a target date for collecting information and phoning for an appointment to meet about May 15.

4. We changed the RE: heading from:
    "Re: Trial"
to
    "Re: Preparations for May 23 Trial"

SPECTOR, SPECTOR & SPECTOR

April 26, 1995

Mrs. Julia Garcia
15 Wedgewood Place
Cow Hollow, NY 10567

Re: Preparations for May 23 Trial

Dear Julia:

Can you get the following information to me by May 5? I need to prepare a
financial statement for the court. I'd like to meet with you before the May
23 trial date, so call me by May 15 to set up a date.

For the financial statement I will need:

1. A realistic appraisal of the property at 15 Wedgewood Place prepared
   by a real estate broker and based on the sale price of comparable
   residences in the area during the last six months.
2. If you and Mr. Garcia cannot agree on an evaluation and division: a
   list of all furniture and furnishings including appliances, silver,
   dishes, crystal, etc. showing the purchase price, date of
   acquisition, and your estimate of present value.
3. An evaluation of the Chevrolet and Edsel.
4. Evaluations of any other properties you consider worth the Court's
   consideration.
5. The balances owing on these properties—if any—as of September 5, 1992
   and May 1, 1995.
6. The source of the money Mr. Garcia used to buy the 1992 Cadillac after
   you separated.
7. Receipts or canceled checks substantiating the $5,700 spent for flood
   repair.

For discussion when we meet

1. Your private agreement to keep the Bentley and assume the balance of
   the $6,563 purchase loan from the First National Bank of Happy Valley.
2. Your agreement to assume half the responsibility for a $3,100 debt to
   Charles Ramirez.

Very truly yours,

JOHN L. SPECTOR
Attorney at Law

Your Perfect Letter Checklist

☑ **BE BRIEF**

Long letters are sometimes unavoidable, but most letters can be considerably improved by shortening. Yes, it's more work to write a short letter than a long one, but the overall savings can be considerable. Even thirty seconds spent pruning and tightening your letter can save:

- your readers' time
- errors—readers are less likely to miss key points
- secretarial time, paper, ink, file space, postage, trees, petroleum products—all our nation's resources
- your reputation—you are seen as more decisive, clear-thinking, efficient, and as a good communicator

Once you get in the habit of eliminating redundancies, obfuscations, and out-of-date phrases, they will disappear from your exploratory writing and you will find your own thinking clarified.

Don't be afraid to write a short letter. Long, hard-to-interpret letters aren't really friendly. You can make your brief notes informative and pleasant, not insultingly abrupt. Short letters are more forceful and effective than effusive, meandering messages.

CHAPTER 9

Asking for a Decision

How often have you received a letter that outlined a problem or offered lots of information and then stopped? The inference was that you would be smart enough to realize that you were supposed to make a decision about how to proceed. Or that you would wade through lots of material to discover and make a coherent list of your options.

Be kinder to *your* readers. When you ask for a decision, set out the reader's options clearly. If you recommend one option over the others, state that up front.

SPECTOR ASSOCIATES

July 13, 1998

Mr. Douglas Daniger
Bushman, Daniger & Novarro
555 S. Flower St.
Los Angeles, CA 99999

Subject: Debt forgiveness
Issue: Capital loss vs. ordinary loss

Dear Doug:

I have spoken with our tax partner, Lee Verily, and he has advised me that the above issue is a complex issue that cannot be easily determined.

On the surface, since WorldWide Wickets' future is tenuous and liquidation is a possibility, debt forgiveness would be recommended rather than a capital contribution. A capital contribution would not be considered 1244 stock. Therefore it would not qualify as an ordinary loss.

If Croquet Masters, Inc. forgives the debt, what kind of loss can he claim— ordinary or capital loss? In order for Croquet Masters to take an ordinary deduction rather than a capital loss, he will have to prove that the investment was made for personal gain rather than to increase the strength of the business.

A decision should be made strictly from a personal point of view. WorldWide Wickets will probably not generate any taxable income since the loss for the current year will probably exceed the note.

Call if you have questions.

If Croquet Masters wants Spector Associates to do additional research, he should contact us.

Very truly yours,

Allan Dwan

WHAT TO DO

Frequently the writer is too close to the material. A letter like this one—with parts of logical pairs missing and terms not defined—often results.

1. What decision should Croquet Masters be asked to make? Write it out here as an "either . . . or" statement.

2. One of Croquet Masters' options requires further decision between two more options. List them here:
    a.
    b.

3. Underline the writer's recommendation.

4. Suggest headings to walk the reader through the choices.

5. Rewrite the subject heading to make it more informative.

WHAT WE DID

ANSWERS

1. Croquet Masters should be asked to choose between debt forgiveness or a capital contribution.

2. One of Croquet Masters' options, debt forgiveness, requires a further decision between two more options:
   a. Ordinary loss
   b. Capital loss

3. The writer's recommendation seems to be in the fourth paragraph:
   "A decision should be made strictly from a personal point of view."

4. For headings to help the reader through the choices, we have chosen:
   "Recommendation" (although it seems weak)
   "Capital Contribution"
   "Debt Forgiveness" (with subheads for "Ordinary loss" and "Capital loss")

5. Our subject heading includes the names of the parties and the requested action.

OUR REWRITE

We have indicated that the reader may be helped by having further information about the advantages and disadvantages of ordinary and capital loss.

SPECTOR ASSOCIATES

July 13, 1998

Mr. Douglas Daniger
Bushman, Daniger & Novarro
555 S. Flower St
Los Angeles, CA 99999

Subject: Croquet Masters' Decision on WorldWide Wickets' debt

Dear Doug:

Our tax partner, Lee Verily, says that Croquet Masters' choice between a capital contribution and debt forgiveness is complex and cannot be decided easily.

Recommendation: Because no clear benefits stand out for either choice, Croquet Masters should choose on a personal basis.

Capital Contribution: Debt forgiveness would probably be preferable to a capital contribution because WorldWide Wickets' future is tenuous and liquidation is a possibility. A capital contribution would not be considered 1244 stock and therefore would not qualify as an ordinary loss.

Debt Forgiveness: WorldWide Wickets will probably not generate any taxable income because the loss for the current year will probably exceed the note. If Croquet Masters chooses to forgive the debt, they could claim either ordinary or capital loss.

- Ordinary loss: To take an ordinary deduction rather than a capital loss, Croquet Masters will have to prove that the investment was made to strengthen the business, not for personal gain. [List any advantages or disadvantages here.]
- Capital loss: If ordinary loss cannot be proven, Croquet Masters will have to take a capital loss. [List any advantages or disadvantages here.]

If Croquet Masters wants Spector Associates to do additional research, they should call us at (415) 777-5555.

Very truly yours,

Allan Dwan

S.S. FINANCIAL

January 2, 1996

Stanley Stanleyson
1234 Sunnyside St.
Spector, CA 90000

SUBJECT: PFF Loan #1111111

Dear Mr. Stanleyson:

Per our conversation of January 2, 1996, enclosed are three adjusted trust
fund analyses.

    A) This analysis is based on a five-month shortage spread. This would pay
       off the shortage by July 1997, when your next regular analysis is due.
       This is our usual procedure for all shortages.

    B) This analysis is based on a 12-month shortage spread. This would pay
       off the shortage by March 1997.

    C) This analysis is based on a 24-month shortage spread. This would pay
       off the shortage by March 1998.

All these analyses are based on a beginning payment of March 1, 1996,
allowing you 45 days in which to look over the information and decide how you
would like to handle this.

There are three additional options open to you.

    A) Pay off the entire shortage amount in a single payment.

    B) Pay off a portion of the shortage amount and request a reanalysis
       based on the remaining amount.

    C) Refinance the property and pay off the shortage as part of the new
       loan. If you refinance with a conventional loan, with a loan-to-value
       ratio of less than 80 percent, you may have the possibility of paying
       your own insurance and taxes.

I spoke with Tom Smith, Manager of Customer Service, and Joe Jones,
Assistant Vice President of Loan Servicing, about your loan. They both
recommend a maximum shortage spread of 24 months. A longer shortage spread
would cause a new shortage to occur within this account.

Please contact me with your decision by March 1, 1996. Should you have any
further questions, please contact me at the above address.

Very truly yours,

S. Spector
Customer Service Representative

Encl.

WHAT TO DO

Assume that the reader of this letter has some financial savvy. (The writer is trying to be helpful by spelling out every possible option.) However, the format doesn't convey the information very clearly. For example, the writer starts right in describing various shortage spreads without indicating that other possibilities exist. A hasty reader might not find the other choices.

1. Put a star next to the three basic options.
2. Put a check next to the three additional options.
3. Underline the request for action. Would you move it?
4. Decide what characteristics the three enclosed analyses have in common. How could you format this information to make comparisons easier?

5. Suggest some headings to divide the information.

WHAT WE DID

ANSWERS

1. The three basic options are described in the attached analyses:

   - Analysis A—a 5-month shortage spread schedule
   - Analysis B—a 12-month shortage spread schedule
   - Analysis C—a 24-month shortage spread schedule

2. The three additional options are:

   - Pay off entirely
   - Pay off a portion
   - Refinance the property

3. The request for action—"Please contact me with your decision"—is in the last paragraph of the Original. We have moved it to the first paragraph.

4. The three enclosed analyses each describe a shortage spread and a payoff date. We have arranged the information in a chart format.

5. We have used headings:

   - "Recommendation"
   - "Three Payment Options"
   - "Three Additional Options"

OUR REWRITE

We have added an easy-to-spot phone number in the closing paragraph. Enclosures are itemized at the bottom of the letter.

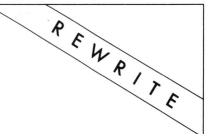

S.S. FINANCIAL

January 2, 1996

Stanley Stanleyson
1234 Sunnyside St.
Spector, CA 90000
SUBJECT: Your payoff options, Loan # 1111111

Dear Mr. Stanleyson:

Here are three adjusted trust fund analyses showing payment options on this loan. Three other payoff options are listed below. Please contact me with your decision before March 1.

Recommendation: Both Tom Smith, Manager of Customer Service, and Joe Jones, Assistant Vice President of Loan Servicing, recommend a maximum shortage spread of 24 months. Even though the 5-month spread is usual, they feel that the longer shortage spread is justified. However, extending it any further would almost certainly cause a new shortage to occur within the account.

Attached analyses	Shortage spread	Paid off by
Analysis A	5 months	July 1996
Analysis B	12 months	March 1997
Analysis C	24 months	March 1988

These analyses are based on making the first payment on March 1, 1996. This allows you at least 45 days to make your decision.

Three Additional Options

1. Pay off the entire shortage in a single payment.
2. Pay off a portion of the shortage amount and request a re-analysis based on the remaining amount due.
3. Refinance the property and pay off the shortage as part of the new loan. If you refinance with a conventional loan that has a loan-to-value ratio of less than 80 percent, you may possibly pay your taxes and insurance.

Please call me at (999) 555-1111 if I can help.

Very truly yours,

S. Spector

Encl: Three adjusted trust fund analyses

CITY OF SPECTORVILLE

March 10, 1997

Ms. Margaret Hamilton
Housing and Human Resources Department
City Hall, Room 700
Spectorville, KS 58792

Dear Ms. Hamilton:

HUD has reminded us that April is traditionally designated as Fair Housing
Month. I believe the City Council made this designation in 1991, but not
since then. As we have the Fair Housing Seminars, which are part of the
educational program associated with the Handicapped Services Audit,
scheduled to start in April, there would appear to be some PR value in the
attached proclamation. Also attached is the first letter from the Mayor and
the representatives of the other involved organizations, which will be sent
to every owner of rental property in Spectorville. The seminar meeting
schedule is on the back of the letter.

It would seem most appropriate for the request for this proclamation to come
from your office. Since the first meeting in April will be on the seventh and
that meeting may, I understand, be canceled because of the election, it
might be best to schedule the proclamation for March 24.

If your office is interested in presenting this proclamation to the City
Council, please call me by March 17. If you approve, I will prepare your
department's Report to the Council for your signature.

Sincerely,

Billie Burke
Community Liaison
Office of the Mayor

WHAT TO DO

How long is it going to take the reader to find out why this writer is writing? The exact purpose is never stated in the letter, only implied!

1. This writer is asking for a decision. Write an opening sentence that requests and describes the decision.

2. Underline any important dates or deadlines. Move them so they follow your opening sentence.

3. Circle any background information that the reader needs to help reach a decision. Write a possible heading for this information.

WHAT WE DID

ANSWERS

1. The opening sentence of the Rewrite opposite asks the reader for a decision:

   "Would you like to declare April 'Fair Housing Month' in Spectorville?"

2. The important dates in the original are:

   - March 17—deadline for notifying writer of approval
   - March 19—City Council meeting
   - March 24—potential date for proclamation

   We've listed the most immediate deadline—the date by which the reader should respond if she agrees—in the second paragraph. The other dates appear in "Scheduling" under "BACKGROUND."

3. The background information is indented under BACKGROUND with appropriate subject subheadings.

OUR REWRITE

We have listed the enclosures. The information about dates that are irrelevant has been eliminated.

CITY OF SPECTORVILLE

March 10, 1997

Ms. Margaret Hamilton
Housing and Human Resources Department
City Hall, Room 700
Spectorville, KS 58792

Dear Ms. Hamilton:

Would you like to declare April ''Fair Housing Month'' in Spectorville? A sample proclamation is attached.

If you approve, call me by March 17, and I will prepare your department's Report to the Council for your signature before the City Council's March 19 meeting.

BACKGROUND

History: HUD has reminded us that April is traditionally designated as Fair Housing Month. I believe the City Council made this designation in 1991, but hasn't done so since.

Tie-in with Fair Housing Seminars: The seminars, which are part of the educational program associated with the Handicapped Services Audit, are scheduled to start in April. There would be some PR value in the attached proclamation. Also attached is the first letter from the Mayor and the representatives of the other involved organizations, which will be sent to every owner of rental property in Spectorville.

Who Should Request Proclamation? It would seem most appropriate for the request for this proclamation to come from your office.

Scheduling: The press conference on March 24 would be a good time to make any announcement, so this proclamation would have to be approved at the March 19 City Council meeting.

Sincerely,

Billie Burke
Community Liaison
Office of the Mayor

Encl: Sample proclamation
      Fair Housing letter and schedule

Your Perfect Letter Checklist

☑ USE RE: IF APPROPRIATE

"Re" is Latin for "in the matter of" or "in reference to." You can often position the reader (and make it easier to retrieve a specific letter later) by listing the subject of your letter on a separate line after the reader's address and before the salutation. (A salutation is the line where you greet your reader: "Dear Ms. Smith.") Start this descriptive phrase with "RE:"—or "SUBJ:" if you prefer.

RE: Your P.O. # 4960, 2/18/97

or:

SUBJ: Christmas Delivery Schedule

If you use such a heading, you do not need to repeat "your purchase order listed above" or "the above matter" in the body of the letter. Choose one or the other. Use RE: whenever it makes the letter *easier* to read and understand, rather than more cluttered.

CHAPTER 10

Complaints

A Perfect Letter can straighten out problems quickly and efficiently. A letter of complaint is the drill sergeant of business correspondence: analyzing and correcting errors, keeping everyone on their toes, pointing our deficiencies, and urging us to do better next time. Good business depends on a good complaint letter—clear, accurate, and justified.

If you are writing a complaint, your purpose is probably one or more of the following:

- You want a past problem to be acknowledged and resolved.
- You want to tell the reader what happened so he can try to prevent this problem in the future.
- You want to feel better.

Start by putting your purpose in the first sentence or paragraph: "We paid for ten motors but you have only shipped us seven." Then list your *supports,* all the details about what is wrong, statistics, dates, previous discussions, etc. Use appropriate headings if they will help the reader's understanding.

Whenever possible, frame the negative in a positive way:

- *not* "The work you did for us is full of mistakes. We cannot accept it and want an immediate refund of our payment to you.
- *but* "Your work is always so good that I was surprised to find some serious problems with your last project. What happened? We had to have it done

over at the last minute by another firm. How can we straighten this out?

The first example establishes that you and the reader are now adversaries. The second assumes that the reader will be your ally in solving the problem. The reader may even be eager to refund your payment as part of the immediate problem-solving process, rather than grudgingly repaying it years from now after expensive, unpleasant legal negotiations.

Assume good intentions. Write as if the flaw was in the execution.

COMPLAINT DO'S

Describe facts

- "The wall unit is two inches shorter than we ordered."
- "The broken motors arrived in unreinforced shipping containers with no internal padding or supports."

Describe feelings

- "I am dismayed and frustrated that this same error has continued to appear on our bill."

Describe what you want

- "We would like the doors refinished and the locks replaced by November 1."
- "Please adjust your July 6 invoice to show a $20,340. credit for the following reasons."

COMPLAINT DON'TS

Don't label

- "Whoever packed this was incompetent." (He is incompetent.)
- "Why is she the only one who never finishes on time?" (She is lazy or inept.)
- "Any resonably intelligent person could have seen that that wouldn't work." (The person responsible is stupid.)

Don't blame

- "Our orders haven't been right since Fred took over."
- "If Gilda would pay more attention to the Illinois accounts, this never would have happened."
- "I've told them over and over, but they can't remember anything."

Don't ridicule

- "I could get better schematic drawings letting a flock of pigeons walk across my desk."

ORIGINAL

SPECTOR CORPORATION

January 15, 1992

Mr. Bruce Larraby
Commercial Life & Casualty
One Parker Place
Seattle, WA 99900

Re: Overpayment Letters

Dear Bruce:

Incredible as it seems, we are still getting letters without sufficient data to respond. As mentioned in past correspondence, we do not have the time to pass these back and forth; therefore, I am requesting that all <u>overpayment</u> and <u>underpayment</u> letters be sent to someone in your office to double-check for accuracy before forwarding to SPECTOR. Please advise regarding this request.

As for the two attachments, we require the location and location number before we can respond. Also, we would prefer knowing the exact amount of overpayment. The letter regarding S. Maxon states that the overpayment is not truly known.

Please have these forwarded to my attention when the information is completed.

Finally, we prepared a matrix of all plants and plans in an effort to clarify location codes. We sent you a copy in mid-December. Perhaps the local Commercial offices could benefit from the information related to their area of responsibility.

Thank you for assisting us with this problem.

Sincerely,

Rachel Zimmerman
Manager of Health and Welfare Plans

Attachments (2)

WHAT TO DO

This overly polite letter fails to make clear what steps the reader should take to solve a continuing problem. The reader may not grasp everything he is being asked to do.

Let's outline the procedures clearly and ask for action directly, although still politely.

1. Put a check next to each thing the reader is being asked to do.

2. Would numbering the requests you have checked help the reader? Would you number them in order of importance? Or in the order in which they should be done?

3. Put a star next to each piece of information the writer wants to receive about overpayment letters.

4. What two pieces of information are missing from this letter?

WHAT WE DID

ANSWERS

1. The things the reader is being asked to do are numbered in our Rewrite.
2. The numbers suggest the order in which they should be done.
3. Overpayment letters need

   - the location
   - the location number

   The writer is also requesting some immediate specific information about S. Maxon.
4. A response phone number and a listing of enclosures are missing.

SPECTOR CORPORATION

January 15, 1992

Mr. Bruce Larraby
Commercial Life & Casualty
One Parker Place
Seattle, WA 99900

RE: Proofreading Overpayment Letters

Dear Bruce:

Incredible as it seems, we are still getting letters without sufficient data for us to respond.

Please do the following:

1. Add the missing information to the two enclosed letters and return them to my attention, by return mail if possible. We need:

- the location for each
- the location number for each
- also the exact amount of S. Maxon's overpayment if possible

2. Appoint someone in your office to proofread all overpayment and underpayment letters before forwarding them to Spector. This will save us both a lot of time now spent passing letters back and forth.

3. Be sure everyone in your Commercial offices has a copy of the matrix of location codes we sent you in December and knows how to use it. That may save us both a lot of time.

Thank you for your help in clearing up this problem.

Sincerely,

Rachel Zimmerman (1-999) 555-4444
Manager of Health and Welfare

Attachments: S. Maxon overpayment letter
              C. Chierichetti overpayment letter

SPECTOR, INC.

September 9, 1998

Jetline Bus Company
223 Griswald Street
Torrence, NH 00998
Attn: Dina

Dear Dina:

To say we were disappointed in the service we received when we rented a van from you on August 30, 1998, would be an understatement.

We had made specific arrangements with you for the van to be here promptly at 10:45 for an 11:00 departure. As you know, the van did not actually arrive until 11:20 and departed at 11:30. The people on the van were scheduled to go to Spectorville for a plant tour and lunch and had to be back at 1:00. Needless to say they had a <u>very</u> rushed tour followed by an <u>extremely</u> rushed lunch and arrived back here at approximately 1:20, throwing off our afternoon schedule.

The other incident that was cause for great consternation on the part of the passengers in the van was that the van arrived at the Eddy Street location and dropped them off quite a distance from the main entrance. Then the driver ''sped off,'' according to the passengers. They then had to walk some distance to the entrance. In addition, they were very concerned all the time they were in Spectorville that they would not know where to meet the driver for the return trip. This concern led to several phone calls back and forth between them and us and your company.

I assume that you agree that, in light of these problems, an adjustment is appropriate. Therefore, I am recommending that there be no charge to us for this date.

Yours very truly,

Helen Vinson
Senior Convention Co-ordinator

WHAT TO DO

This is a pretty good Original letter. The writer starts with an overview of the problem (although not the requested resolution) and details why the service was unsatisfactory. Let's polish it, to create a Perfect Letter.

1. Move the requested adjustment to the opening paragraph.

2. Put a check next to each complaint and list them with appropriate headings here:

WHAT WE DID

ANSWERS

1. We have moved the requested adjustment to the opening paragraph.

2. We have listed three major complaints under the group heading "Problems." The rushed tour and lunch—certainly a reason for complaint—are a result of the late arrival, so we have described them under that heading.

SPECTOR, INC.

September 9, 1998

Jetline Bus Company
223 Griswald Street
Torrence, NH 00998
Attn: Dina

Dear Dina:

We were extremely disappointed with the service we received when we rented a van from you on August 30, 1998. We request an adjustment and feel that there should be no charge to us for this rental.

Problems

Van was 35 minutes late. We made specific arrangements with you for the van to arrive promptly at 10:45 for an 11:00 departure. The van did not arrive until 11:20 and we departed at 11:30.

As a result the scheduled plant tour and lunch for the passengers were extremely rushed and they still returned 20 minutes late, throwing off our afternoon schedule.

Passengers dropped off at inconvenient location. Although the driver let our people off on Eddy Street, the street the plant is on, they were more than four blocks from the main entrance. This caused them concern, confusion, and a long walk.

Driver did not set return pickup site. The passengers reported that the driver ''sped off'' without telling them where they would be picked up for the return trip. Their concern marred their concentration on activities there and led to several phone calls back and forth between them, us, and your company.

Please let me know how you propose to handle this.

Yours very truly,

Helen Vinson
Senior Convention Co-ordinator

SPECTOR SAVINGS

May 27, 1996

Ms. Mae Marsh
Spector Savings
P.O. Box 777
Spectorville, CA 90000

Dear Ms. Marsh:

Per our conversation of today, please find enclosed copies of a letter and two verifications for Loan #2222222 for David Wark Griffith. Our letter of inquiry concerning the large discrepancy in the loan amounts and monthly payments verified for the same loan was mailed May 13.

As we had not heard back from you, I phoned Spector Saving today and got transferred to several different departments. I learned that this loan was paid off and that you had no record of receiving a letter from us concerning the differences reported for loan amounts. You asked me to send additional copies of the two verifications in question to your attention so that you could research it for us.

I'm sure you can understand our concern. We need to clear this up as soon as possible, as a loan decision is pending. We would like an explanation for the differences in reported loan balances for the same loan. We would also like to know if the people verifying the loan balances were authorized to do so. Are they both employees in the Spectorville office or is one of them an employee of the Culver County branch of Spector Savings?

Please send your written response to my attention in INTERNAL AUDIT. Feel free to call me at (415) 555-5555 if you need further information for your research.

Sincerely,

Robert Harron
Internal Audit

Encl.

cc: Dorothy Gish
    Richard Barthelmess

WHAT TO DO

This letter gets all tangled up in the past, the present, and the future. The writer is making a complicated situation even more complicated. We can almost hear the reader despairing: "What does this person want from me?"

1. Put a check next to each thing the writer wants from the reader.

2. Suggest categories for these requests

3. Suggest an opening paragraph that will ask clearly for what is wanted.

4. There is a lot of background material in this letter. How could it be handled for the benefit of the reader?

5. What is missing from this letter?

WHAT WE DID

ANSWERS

1. The four requests are listed under the first two headings of our Rewrite.

2. We have divided the information under the first two headings.

3. Our opening paragraph asks for an explanation of discrepancies on the account listed in the RE: heading.

4. Background material is listed under the heading "Background."

5. Missing from the letter are:

   - the address where the reply should be sent
   - a listing of enclosures

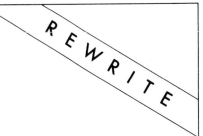

SPECTOR SAVINGS

May 27, 1996

Ms. Mae Marsh
Spector Savings
P.O. Box 777
Spectorville, CA 90000

                    RE: <u>Discrepancies—Loan #2222222</u>
                        David Wark Griffith

Dear Ms. Marsh:

I need a speedy explanation for the large discrepancies in loan amount and
monthly payments reported on this account. As you and I discussed today, we
must clear this up promptly because a new loan decision is pending.

<u>I need to know</u>:

 1. Why are different loan balances reported for the same loan?
 2. Were the two people who verified the different loan balances both
     authorized to do so?
 3. Are they both employees in the Spectorville office or is one of them an
     employee of a Culver County branch of Spector Savings?

<u>Use enclosed form to reply</u>:

Fill out the verification form in duplicate and return to me as soon as you
have completed your research.

<u>Background</u>: I wrote you on May 13, 1996, about this problem but received no
reply. I phoned Spector Savings today and was transferred to several
different departments. I learned that this loan has been paid off and that
you had no record of receiving our letter. You asked for additional copies of
the two verifications so you could research it for us.

<u>Reply to</u>: INTERNAL AUDIT, Attn. Robert Harron. Feel free to call me at (415)
555-5555 if you need further information.

Sincerely,

Robert Harron
Internal Audit

Encl: Copy of 5/13 inquiry letter
      Two (2) verification forms

cc: Dorothy Gish
    Richard Barthelmess

CHAPTER 11

Condolences

Writing a letter of condolence is not easy for most people. Those written in business situations can be especially difficult when you worked with the deceased but don't know the person to whom you are writing the condolence letter, or you are writing to an employee who has lost a close relative, someone you didn't know well or at all.

How much can be said at a time like this? Being too brief may sound cold and uncaring. Running on and on or being very effusive may sound insincere.

Suppose that you are called on to write to the survivors of an employee you knew only by sight, or someone who had been with your firm for a very short time. What should you say? What should you *not* say?

O'HERLIHY, EPSTEIN & DELGADO

October 22, 1995

Mrs. Eduardo Suarez
210 Lindor Avenue
Long Beach, TX 54708

Dear Mrs. Suarez:

I and all of us here at O'Herlihy, Epstein & Delgado were saddened by the news
last Friday of the death of our beloved colleague. We were just starting the
morning partnership meeting, and all of us felt terrible when we heard.

No one knows what to say or what comfort to offer at a time like this.
Probably nothing we say can help you very much. Anyway, we wanted you to know
that we are thinking of you.

Eduardo's contribution to the firm will long be remembered, and all who knew
him will remember him as a hard-working, fair-minded attorney.

As you may know, Eduardo is covered by several company insurance policies
payable to the company. Also you, as his widow, have a claim to some benefits
from his share as partner. When you have the time, would you bring a copy of
his death certificate to Miss McGinley in Personnel, room 1402, to help us
start processing our claims? Someone from our office will be in touch with
you soon about Eduardo's partnership claims. Would you also bring birth
certificates for your children and your marriage license? We will do what we
can to help you with the paperwork.

Again, accept our sympathy, Mrs. Suarez, and remember, if we can do anything
to be of help, please let me know.

With sympathy,

Peter Pinto
Partner

WHAT TO DO

How many sympathy letters have you written in which you said "I don't know what to say"? It's a pretty standard human reaction. This letter writer obviously meant well, sending a sort of stream-of-consciousness monologue of everything going through his mind.

Let's assume that this writer is writing to a widow he never met. How can he improve this letter?

1. Underline what you, as the receiver of this letter, would probably find comforting.

2. Circle what you, as the receiver of this letter, might respond to negatively. What would you delete?

3. Is there anything you would add to this letter?

WHAT WE DID

ANSWERS

1. The reader will probably find little comfort in the Original letter, other than knowing perhaps that Eduardo's death made others feel terrible.

2. The reader may respond negatively to detailed financial instructions. Save them for a later communication (and make them much more clear—see the Divorce Trial Inventory letter on page 69 for tips on giving instructions to someone under stress).

   The reader may also respond negatively to the somewhat impersonal tone of:

   "Eduardo's contribution to the firm will long be remembered, and all who knew him will remember him as a hard-working, fair-minded attorney."

3. We have chosen to add some personal reminiscences to the letter.

OUR REWRITE

When you send a condolence letter and don't know the deceased well, pretend you have been hired to write an obituary or prepare a eulogy. Do some research. Talk to others if possible. Then in your letter concentrate on accomplishments that have affected or helped others, happy remembrances, the characteristics that will be remembered. (Here is where death should transform harsh adjectives into gentler ones: the person who was rigid becomes "principled"; the rude become "discriminating" and "outspoken"; the foul-mouthed become "eloquent manipulators of the English language," etc.)

We have imagined that the writer of this condolence letter did his homework and gathered some reminiscences about the deceased that may comfort the reader now and be reread with pleasure later.

O'HERLIHY, EPSTEIN & DELGADO

October 22, 1995

Mrs. Eduardo Suarez
210 Lindor Avenue
Long Beach, TX 54708

Dear Mrs. Suarez:

We had just started the Friday morning partnership meeting when we heard about Eduardo's death. We were all extremely saddened. Many of the old-timers recalled working with Eduardo in the early days of O'Herlihy, Epstein & Delgado, when Eduardo was a junior associate under Vincent Delgado—how Eduardo made his reputation as one of the hardest working, most competent young lawyers in Texas. Vincent, Jr. recalled several stories his father used to tell about his adventures with Eduardo when they set up pro bono legal clinics in the 1950s, and how Mr. Delgado always said that it was Eduardo's tenacity and refusal to give up that made the clinics a success.

We are really going to miss Eduardo's vision, his energy, his grace under pressure, and his special sense of humor. We know how proud he was of his family. Your photos covered most of the walls in his office, and he joked that if he had any more grandchildren, he'd have to get a bigger office.

I've talked to several of the new associates who were under Eduardo and each of them had a special story to tell me of his kindness and his skill in getting the best from those he worked with. Everyone at OE&D was very proud of Eduardo Suarez. The contributions he made to his firm, to the community, and to the legal system of Texas will not be forgotten.

We are eager to be of any help we can to you and your family. Please call on me for any assistance you may need. When you feel up to it, you can get in touch with Phyllis McGinley, ext. 339, for information about Eduardo's partnership benefits and other financial matters.

With sympathy,

Peter Pinto
Partner

SPECTOR CORPORATION

October 11, 1997

Mr. Paul Rubens
77 Herman Place
Alamo, TX 57783

Dear Mr. Rubens,

On behalf of Spector Corporation, may I offer you our heartfelt condolences on the death of your son.

Although we can't say much that will comfort you at a time like this, we want you to know that you have our deepest sympathy.

Sincerely,

Frances Buxton
Vice President

WHAT TO DO

This is a typical, straightforward, and fairly good condolence letter sent by a busy vice president of a large company to a worker in the shipping department.

Let us assume that this vice president or her secretary does some research before writing and learns that: (a) the dead son had been a grief to his family, in and out of trouble, and died from a drug overdose; or (b) that the son had a terrible terminal disease for several years before his death; or (c) the child died of sudden infant death syndrome.

1. Make a list here of at least three things the writer of a business condolence letter should *not* say in response to any of these tragic situations:
    a.
    b.
    c.

2. Circle any phrases in the Original that might sound "trite" or "formula."

WHAT WE DID

ANSWERS

1. A few of the statements that would be inappropriate in a business condolence letter are:
   "It was God's will.
   "It must be a relief to know that he isn't suffering any more."
   "Hopefully you can have another child soon."

2. Some clichés in the Original are:
   "On behalf of Spector Corporation"
   "may I offer"
   "our heartfelt condolences"
   "on the death of"
   "at a time like this"
   "we want you to know that"
   "you have our deepest sympathy"

OUR REWRITE

We have tried to craft a simple statement of support, skipping as many cliches as possible. The quick research done on this sad event should also have revealed the child's name, whether Paul Ruben had a wife living with him, and, if so, what her name was. We have added these names to the letter.

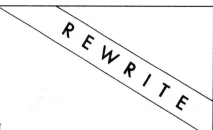

SPECTOR CORPORATION

October 11, 1997

Mr. Paul Rubens
77 Herman Place
Alamo, TX 57783

Dear Paul,

You and your wife Simone have all our sympathy for the loss of your son
Jeremy. Your friends and coworkers here at Spector send you their profound
condolences.

Sincerely,

Frances Buxton
Vice President

Your Perfect Letter Checklist

☑ **DESCRIBE ANY ENCLOSURES**

Always list what you are enclosing. Don't just type "Encl." or "ENC:" at the bottom of your letters. Give a *brief* description, especially if you haven't already described the enclosures in the letter.

"Encl: 1998 Profit Report"

or

"ENC: copies 11/19/99 letter
1/21/98 letter
5/9/97 letter"

Why take the time to do this when it should be obvious what is in the envelope? Because letters are often records of who said what to whom and who knew what when. Besides, the thirty seconds spent can save you lots of time and headaches later.

- It helps you or your secretary assemble *all* the contents before you seal the envelope.
- It provides you with an exact record if a question occurs later.
- It ensures that your readers are aware of exactly what they should have received.

CHAPTER 12

Congratulations

Letters of congratulations take so little time compared to the good they can do. We all like to receive sincere praise and thanks, even one-liners. One executive, writing to a prominent businessman after a promotion, kept his note to one word: "WOW!" He got a personal call of thanks.

The key to a good letter of congratulations is sincerity and the mark of sincerity is brevity. Say what you feel in a few honest words and your comments will be deeply appreciated.

SPECTOR MANAGEMENT COMPANY

November 20, 1995

Mr. Larry Parks
Cantor, Jolson & Williams Assoc.
1550 Broadway
New York, NY 10025

Dear Mr. Parks,

While I was reading the Business Section of the _Times_ yesterday, my eye caught the article stating that you were elected president of the Shubert Alley Merchants' Association.

This is a well-respected group which has had many prominent presidents in past years. I have been happy to work with both their current president, Al Simington, and the former president, Sheila Broadbent. The organization has a long and prestigious record for accomplishment which I hope you will carry on.

I will be looking forward to great things under your leadership next year. Best of luck and congratulations.

Cordially yours,

Betty Garrett

WHAT TO DO

This is a sincere but misdirected and awkward letter of congratulations.

1. Underline the sentences that praise the reader and offer congratulations.
2. Circle any information that should be rephrased or deleted.

Wᴏᴀᴛ ᴡᴇ ᴅɪᴅ

ANSWERS

1. The sentence that praises the reader is the final one, preceded by four general information sentences.

2. Much of the general information should be deleted or reframed as supports for the congratulatory message. See our Rewrite.

THE SPECTOR GROUP

November 20, 1995

Mr. Larry Parks
Cantor, Jolson & Williams Assoc.
1550 Broadway
New York, NY 10025

Dear Mr. Parks,

I was delighted to read in the New York Times yesterday that you had been
elected president of the Shubert Alley Merchant's Association.

What a coup for the Association to get you! Still, they have always managed
to attract top people, and I am confident that you will surpass anything done
by your illustrious predecessors.

Congratulations and good luck.

Cordially,

Betty Garrett

Your Perfect Letter Checklist

☑ CHECK THE "TONE"

One of the most subtle and difficult-to-master characteristics of a letter is the tone. Tone in a letter is what attitude is in a person. Most American business letters today assume a friendly, slightly (but-not-too) casual tone, free of archaic phrases and jargon, with a simplicity and directness of style. This is the tone you will be practicing in *The Perfect Letter*. This may or may not be the right tone for you, your company, or your immediate message. The important thing is that you learn to recognize and adapt your tone to the situation, just as you adapt the tone of your voice and your manner of speech to different occasions.

The tone of your letters should be as deliberately chosen as your words. It can vary, depending on the subject and the intended reader. If your letter is perceived by the reader as being condescending, antagonistic, indecisive, effusive, or having any other usually undesirable tones, that should be a political choice on your part, not an accident.

If you're not quite sure what *tone* is, here are several ways to say the same thing:

- "This is to inform you of our new closing time."
- "We are pleased to announce our new extended hours."
- "Bill, I thought you'd like to know that from now on we'll be open until 7:00 P.M."
- "New Closing Time: 19:00 hours. Monday through Friday."

Each of these approaches may be appropriate for a particular reader. After you have refined *what* you want to say, you should decide *how* you want to say it—that is, what *tone* is most likely to produce the response you want from your reader.

CHAPTER 13

Follow-ups

Another Perfect Letter power tool is a good follow-up. Follow-up letters can serve a variety of purposes:

- create a written record of what happened (for example at a meeting)
- reinforce what was said (for example, at a sales call)
- evaluate or critique an event to aid future planning
- show your interest (or disinterest)

There are three common traps for less-than-perfect follow-up letters:

1. Waiting so long to respond that any benefit is lost.
2. Writing immediately, but using a computerized form letter, containing few if any details of what happened.
3. Sending stream-of-consciousness notes—Exploratory Phase writing—as a final draft.

Perfect Letter writers realize that good writing is *part* of business, not an intrusion, so they develop the habit of creating individualized follow-up letters.

SPECTOR CORPORATION

January 25, 1998

Mr. Jack Holt
Special Assistant to the President
Middle State University
Middle, MO 65555

Dear Jack:

Just wanted to drop a note regarding Spector's participation at the
''Minority Job Fair'' on Wednesday, 13 January 1998. Lynette Bennett and I
were quite pleased, in fact impressed with the organization/mechanics of
the Job Fair. However, we were a bit disappointed with the physical layout of
the Fair itself. I don't believe there should have been two rooms for company
representatives, and we were somewhat ''cramped'' for space, i.e., there
was poor access for the employers to get out and mingle with the students. I
was impressed with the caliber of the students; I was sorry we didn't have
more opportunities available. We saw a good cross-section of students—
minority/non-minority, men and women. I spoke with a number of students
regarding Spector's 1) financial management program, 2) information systems
management programs, 3) employee relations management program, 4)
manufacturing management program, and the various marketing programs. Our
facility in Kansas City has a number of these programs (on the small side)
but the majority of the opportunities are really outside Missouri. When the
students were informed of this, their interest in the company decreased.
It's a shame that Middle State University does not have an engineering
program, in light of the proximity of the university to nearby engineering
firms. Spector has a number of openings in the engineering field and locally
we have an outstanding training program. Overall, we found the day to be
fruitful and would be interested in participating in future Job Fairs.

Sincerely,

Warren Danskin, Specialist
Professional Resources

WHAT TO DO

This original (don't forget that this is a *real* letter) is twenty-one lines long without an indent.

1. As you read this letter, put a pencil slash wherever the writer changes the subject.

2. Which of the following categories might be used as headings to divide this information?

    ( )   dates that things happened
    ( )   kinds of programs discussed
    ( )   positive and negative points
    ( )   past and future actions
    ( )   who needs to do what

3. What sequence to you suggest for these headings so that they address the needs of the reader? Which would you put first?

4. Would a "RE:" heading at the top help the reader/s now and in the future? If so, jot one here:

WHAT WE DID

ANSWERS

1. See Rewrite for divisions of Original letter into topics.
2. The best category for dividing the material under headings is:
   (X) positive and negative points
3. The reader probably would benefit from knowing the positive points first, then the negative points.
4. We've added a headline:
   RE: Minority Job Fair, January 13, 1998.

OUR REWRITE

Writing headings, even if you don't use them in your final draft, gives you an overview of your communication. This writer opens with how impressed they were, then discusses his most immediate personal concern: their discomfort in the physical space at the Fair. While that is certainly important information to pass on, it should probably come last in his critique.

Notice how easy the crafted version of this letter is to read. Dividing the information into positive and negative points and then adding headings makes the information accessible without being any less friendly.

SPECTOR CORPORATION

January 25, 1998

Mr. Jack Holt
Special Assistant to the President
Middle State University
Middle, MO 65555

RE: Minority Job Fair, January 13

Dear Jack:

Overall, we found the day fruitful at your Minority Job Fair and we would be interested in participating in future job fairs.

POSITIVE POINTS

Organization—Lynette Bennett and I were quite pleased, in fact impressed, with the organization and mechanics of the job fair.

Good cross-section of students—I spoke with a number of minority and non-minority men and women regarding our programs in:

1. financial management
2. information systems management
3. employee relations management
4. manufacturing management
5. marketing

NEGATIVE POINTS

Majority of Spector jobs outside the state—When the students learned this, their interest decreased.

No Engineering program at Middle State—It's a shame, because M.S. is so near major engineering firms. Spector has a number of openings in the engineering field and we have an outstanding local training program.

Physical layout—We were a bit disappointed. One large room would have been better than two smaller ones. We were somewhat cramped for space and there was poor access for us to get out from behind the tables so we could mingle with the students.

Thanks for letting us be part of the Minority Job Fair.

Sincerely,

Warren Danskin, Specialist

ORIGINAL

SPECTOR MAILING SYSTEMS

February 15, 1995

Mrs. Barbara Ling
Compton Synthetics
2 Handley Lane
Longhorn, TX 76444

Dear Mrs. Ling:

It was a pleasure to have met with you and discussed the Jones Monthly
Mailing and Data Processing Systems.

Should you desire further information, please feel welcome to call on me. My
telephone number is 212-387-0685.

Thank you for your continued consideration, and looking forward to being of
service to you, I remain,

Very truly yours,

Carmen Melendez

WHAT TO DO

Form follow-up letters after sales calls or meetings can be deadly dull. Why write them? To go on record that a meeting took place and hopefully to keep the energy going that was begun at the meeting. This impersonal computer-generated original fails on both counts. It says nothing about when the meeting took place and it certainly doesn't show any enthusiasm for this prospective client's concerns.

If you're selling something, always focus on how your product or service can benefit your prospect. Answer the unspoken question: "What's in it for me?" People buy benefits, not products.

1. How would you make this a record of a specific encounter without cluttering up the letter?

2. Take the time to describe how your product can make the reader's life better. Show that you listened to her concerns. (You'll have to make this up.)

3. Close with a sentence that will keep communications open and encourage future contact.

WHAT WE DID

ANSWERS

1. You could say "When we talked Thursday . . ." or "At our meeting yesterday . . ." For this Rewrite, we've added the date as an RE.

2. We've created a fantasy scenario of how this sales-person could respond to information gained during the sales call. If good sleuthing revealed that the prospect's major concern seems to be getting mailing problems under control so she can focus on new sales territories, then this is your "benefit." Show that you listened. Show that you care.

3. The closing sentence of the Original certainly tries to keep the door open in a generic way. We think our Rewrite offers a more immediate reason for the reader to call the writer. Of course, if you hope never to hear from the reader again, stick to a polite formula closing. But if you really want further contact, imagine what would make *you* pick up the phone or schedule a meeting. How pressured do you want the reader to feel about keeping the relationship going? What potential benefits would outweigh the investment of time and the risk of commitment?

SPECTOR MAILING SYSTEMS

February 15, 1995

Mrs. Barbara Ling
Compton Synthetics
2 Handley Lane
Longhorn, TX 76444

Re: Our meeting 2/14/95

Dear Mrs. Ling:

Your mailing problems are certainly complex and I was impressed with how you are handling them in a systematic and orderly way.

The more I have thought over your concerns, the more I am certain that the #500 model of the Jones Monthly Mailing and Data Processing Systems could solve many of the problems you mentioned without increasing your overall monthly costs. This would free you up to concentrate more on your new sales territories.

Please call me any morning at 1-212-387-0685 if you'd like me to explain how this would work for you, or if any more questions have occurred to you.

Sincerely,

Carmen Melendez
SPECTOR MAILING SYSTEMS

Your Perfect Letter Checklist

☑ **SPECIFY TIMES AND DATES**

Whenever possible, avoid phrases like "as soon as possible" or even "urgent." Does "urgent" mean an hour or a month?

Use a specific time or date: "by Thursday," "before December 11," or "in the morning between 9:30 and 11:30 A.M." Use human nature to your advantage by providing clear, concise guidelines for what you expect.

INSTEAD OF:	SAY:
after which time	then
at that point in time	then
at this point in time	now
at a later date	later
in a timely manner	promptly *or* efficiently
at your earliest convenience	as soon as you can
at an early date	give a specific date

CHAPTER 14

Instructions

When you want someone to do something for you, the temptation is to swathe your request in polite language so you don't seem rude. Too often this can obscure what you are really asking for, so both the writer and reader end up frustrated.

Perfect Letter instructions should be clear, logical, concise, chronological if necessary, and impossible to interpret in more than one way. A noted Shakespeare scholar, G. B. Harrison, said he learned more about writing in the army than from all his schooling:

> It is far easier to discuss Hamlet's complexes than to write orders which ensure that five working parties from five different units arrive at the right place at the right time, equipped with proper tools for the job.
>
> One soon learns that the most seemingly simple statement can bear two meanings, and that, when instructions are misunderstood, the fault usually lies with the wording of the original order.

A manager sent a sample of a mailer to a printer: "Copy this exactly and be sure to save the tear-out reply coupon." She wanted to be sure that the coupons would be perforated like the sample. The large mailing went out right on schedule, and the astonished manager was handed a box of blank reply coupons, carefully torn from each mailer by a staff working overtime. Moral: it pays to have another person read over your instructions and tell you what they think you said.

SPECTOR CORPORATION

November 11, 1996

Spector Travel, Inc.
102 Broad Street
Spectorville, NY 11111

Dear Sally:

Enclosed are the tickets for Mr. Sam Hardy, dated for departure of 11/18 and a return of 11/20 from New York to Oshkosh.

The engagement for that date has been canceled. I therefore wish to cancel the enclosed tickets and have a credit issued against Mr. Hardy's Fly-By card, #0043-996-199. Also I wish to have a copy of the credit issued, sent to my attention at the office.

Thanking you in advance,

Sincerely,

SPECTOR CORPORATION

Nadia Westman
Administrative Assistant

WHAT TO DO

Here is a deceptively simple letter. It might get the job done, but it could be rewritten so that it would almost guarantee the reader will understand everything the writer is asking for.

1. Underline any active verbs that describe what the writer wants the reader to do, for example: "Please *return* forms."

2. Circle any verbs that describe requested actions with passive verbs, for example: "The forms should be returned."

3. Put a star next to each action requested.

WHAT WE DID

ANSWERS

1. The Original has no active verbs that describe directly what the writer wants the reader to do. The only active verbs concern the writer: "I . . . *wish* to cancel" and . . . I *wish* to have a copy . . . issued."

2. The passive verbs are:

   - "Enclosed are"
   - "has been canceled"
   - "wish to cancel"
   - "have a credit issued"
   - "have a copy issued [and] sent"

3. The three requested actions are highlighted with asterisks in the Rewrite.

SPECTOR CORPORATION

November 11, 1996

Ms. Sally Blane
Spector Travel, Inc.
102 Broad Street
Spectorville, NY 11111

Dear Sally:

Please help me with the following:
- Cancel the enclosed plane tickets (11/18 departure, 11/20 return, between New York and Oshkosh).
- Issue a credit against Mr. Sam Hardy's Fly-By credit card, #0043-996-199.
- Send a copy of the credit to my attention.

Mr. Hardy's engagement was canceled. Thanks as always for all your help.

Sincerely,

SPECTOR CORPORATION

Nadia Westman
Administrative Assistant

Encl.: Tickets

ORIGINAL

SPECTOR VACATIONS INCORPORATED

February 19, 1997

Mr. Jim Butcher, Manager
ComputerDaze
#1 Spector Road
Spector, CA 99999

Dear Mr. Butcher:

This letter is in reference to the Ad Fund accounts of stores #2004, #6444, and #3808.

It is the request of the Royalty Department that the Ad Fund for these three stores be paid by check rather than by bank wire.

The reason for this is that the monies for bank wires are in the Bank of Toronto and the Ad Fund account for the stores are in Fidelity Bank. Our system cannot support this function of distributing monies from one bank account to another.

It would be greatly appreciated if this request be acted on effective with your next Ad Fund payment.

Thank you.

Nick Brady
Royalty Specialist

cc: R. Thorn

WHAT TO DO

This letter seems straightforward and explicit enough. Why does it need more work? Think again of the amount of time the reader needs to understand and comply with a request. The more we can reduce this time, the more productive the reader can be and the more likely he or she is to respond favorably to our request.

1. The writer's main flaw is using passive verbs so frequently in the hope that they will sound more polite. Underline the instruction in the original. Suggest a new opening sentence that puts that purpose up front.

2. Circle all phrases with passive verbs.

3. Sentences that start with "It . . ." should send up a red flare. Determine to what or whom the two "its" in this Original refer and suggest sentences specifying the actor and the active verb.

WHAT WE DID

ANSWERS

1. The instruction in the original is:

   ``It is the request of the Royalty Department that the Ad Fund for these three stores be paid by check rather than bank wire.''

   The opening sentence of the Rewrite changes the passive "that [it] be paid by check" to the active "Please make Ad Fund payments by check . . ."

2. Some phrases with passive verbs in the Original are:

   - "It is the request of"
   - "be paid by check"
   - "if this request be acted on"

3. "*It* is the request" becomes "*we* request that *you* pay by check"
   "*It* would be greatly appreciated" becomes "*you* acting promptly"

SPECTOR VACATIONS INCORPORATED

February 10, 1997

Mr. Jim Butcher, Manager
ComputerDaze
#1 Spector Road
Spector, CA 99999

Dear Mr. Butcher:

Please make Ad Fund payments by check instead of by bank wire for the
following stores:

    #2004
    #6444
    #3808

Currently, we keep the Ad Fund account with Fidelity Bank, but handle bank
wires through Bank of Toronto. Unfortunately, we did not set up our system to
handle transferring funds from one bank account to the other.

We would be grateful if you could begin this new procedure with your next Ad
Fund payment.

If you have any questions, please call me at extension 2233.

Thank you,

Nick Brady
Royalty Specialist

cc: R. Thorn

SPECTOR ASSOCIATES

September 15, 1996

Ms. Thana Topsis
Customer Service
Vacation Land Enterprises
53 Thoreau Place
Walden, MA 01327

RE: <u>Vacation Land Guest Survey</u>

Dear Thana,

In response to our telephone conversation today, enclosed are copies of the following:

1. A letter from you to all managers informing them of the upcoming survey. This letter should go out to the managers as soon as you wish, but probably no later than October 1.

2. A copy of a letter from R. W. Emerson to all managers giving the instructions for distribution. I have made some changes on it regarding the distribution. Please review this with R. W. This letter goes in the boxes with the questionnaires, so I need this to be retyped on Vacation Land stationery and sent back to me for printing.

3. A memo addressed to all hotel personnel. This memo is also mailed out in the box with the questionnaires for the managers to post and/or instruct their personnel about the survey.

I will get the questionnaire to the printers as soon as possible. Distribution will be November 1 through November 5. As you mentioned in a previous letter, we will delete the hourly schedule for distribution. This should make it easier for the managers.

The cost of the survey in total will be approximately $40,000. This includes the Field Research tabulation and printing.

Will you please get the two items back to me within the next ten days, so that I will have them boxed with the questionnaires.

It will be most helpful if you get a chance to talk to the managers at some point in time about the upcoming survey. Perhaps this would improve the return rate and would give us a little assurance that the managers will in fact distribute them.

Sincerely,

Shelley Keats

Encl.

WHAT TO DO

The neat list of enclosures makes this letter look well thought out, but first impressions can be deceiving.

1. Underline the verbs that describe what the reader is being asked to do.
2.   Put a star next to deadlines that the reader is being asked to meet.
3. Circle other important information.

WHAT WE DID

ANSWERS

1. This was a trick question because two important things the reader is being asked to do have to be guessed from the context:

   - Check the enclosures (*inferred*)
   - Review letter with R. W. Emerson
   - Return corrected letter on letterhead (*inferred*)
   - Return items within three weeks
   - Talk to managers

2. The deadlines the reader is being asked to meet are:

   - "get the two items back to me within the next *ten days* . . ."
   - "This letter should go out . . . no later than *October 1*."

3. Other important information probably includes the dates and cost of the survey.

REWRITE

SPECTOR ASSOCIATES

September 15, 1996

Ms. Thana Topsis
Customer Service
Vacation Lane Enterprises
53 Thoreau Place
Walden, MA 01327

RE: Vacation Land Guest Survey

Dear Thana,

Please check over the enclosed two letters and a memo and have them typed on
Vacation Land stationery.

Send to the managers by October 1:

> Enclosure 1—Letter from you to all managers informing them of upcoming
> survey

Return to me by September 25 for printing:

> Enclosure 2—Copy of a letter from R. W. Emerson to all managers giving
> the instructions for distribution. NOTE: I have made some
> changes in distribution so please review with R. W.

> Enclosure 3—Memo addressed to all hotel personnel. This will be mailed
> to managers in the same box with the questionnaires so
> they can be posted or used to instruct employees about the
> survey.

Please talk to managers if you can. This would probably improve return rate
and give us assurance that the managers will distribute the questionnaire.
As you requested, we are deleting the hourly schedule for distribution which
should make it easier for the managers.

Total cost of survey: $40,000 including Field Research tabulation and
printing.

Distribution Dates: November 1—5

Sincerely,

Shelley Keats

3 Encl.
(described above)

Your Perfect Letter Checklist

☑ **AVOID DATED LANGUAGE**

Most old-style business English is no longer used, but some of it lingers on in legal and political jargon. Use clear contemporary terms. That doesn't mean you have to "dumb down" your writing—just skip phrases that take too much time and energy to express simple ideas.

INSTEAD OF:	SAY:
first of all	first
in the event that	if
in view of the fact that	because
enclosed please find	_____ is enclosed
inform *or* advise	tell *or* say
to my attention	to me
the undersigned *or* the writer *or* yours truly	I *or* me
in the amount of	for $_____
inasmuch as	since *or* because

CHAPTER 15

Newsletters

Organizations sometimes use a letter from the president or director as a sort of newsletter to update outsiders on recent happenings and to maintain contact with people who would not receive an in-house newsletter. These well-intentioned letters are often thinly disguised public relations pieces, but since they don't go through the usual PR channels, where bright, tight writing is a must, they can become fairly heavy reading.

If you are going to create such a progress report for your business in letter form, be sure that it is a Perfect Letter.

CENTRAL COLLEGE

July, 1990

MEMORANDUM:

TO: Alumni, Parents, and Friends

A keen sense of the passing of time is one of those occupational hazards educators come to expect in their profession, but never quite get used to. Late each spring with Commencement, faculty and administrators—the whole College really—officially end another school year, saying good-bye to students and parents we've come to know extraordinarily well. We share with these graduates a feeling of achievement over what has been accomplished and of anticipation for the exciting experiences and careers which lie ahead. Indeed, the class of 1990 holds a very special place in our history. Twenty-five years ago, in 1965, we graduated our first class from the Macklin campus. And seventy years ago, in 1920 we issued our very first liberal arts degrees in a small ceremony at our Boston campus. John Keenon was President then, but I doubt that even he could have foreseen how the College would grow throughout the twenties and thirties and in the decades to come. In just this past year, we've made some remarkable progress—as an institution of higher learning, as an important intellectual resource for the surrounding population, and as a community of individuals.

Perhaps the most tangible progress has been made in the area of financial stability. After a year of negotiations and discussion, the College on May 29 sold 23.4 acres of surplus property to The Spector Company for a new corporate headquarters to replace cramped facilities in downtown Framingham. This move was absolutely essential to the economic future of Sussex County and to the state's plans for retaining and attracting industry. For us, it was a major step forward in our efforts to put the College on a sound financial footing. The quality of the education we offer is a basic ingredient of our institutional life—but it _is_ costly. The sale of this land has eradicated half of our accumulated deficit; without it, our long-term viability would have been in serious question.

Lengthy conversations with Spector's executives have convinced me that their building (designed by the renowned F. I. Takahashi) will complement both the campus and the larger environment. Actually, some of you who have not visited the campus in recent years would probably be amazed at the way the area around Macklin has changed. Over the last ten years, specified parts of Devon, Essex, Newtown, Greenwood, and other towns have been set aside for corporate development, so that today, only a few minutes from the College, are the headquarters of Standard, Korox, JTI, and Siliconica, as well as regional offices for Matsushi, Tarae Publications, and dozens of other companies.

I firmly believe that working with companies such as these is an important part of the College's mission. In the months to come, we anticipate some exciting cooperative ventures which will represent new extensions of our liberal arts mission. We intend, for instance, to establish an ongoing program of work opportunities and internships in area corporations for our undergraduates (more and more of whom choose business as a career). We also hope to begin a modest exchange program between corporate personnel and our own faculty—opening up a marvelous opportunity for give-and-take between a small college and big business, between the world of ideas in academia and the application of theory in commerce and industry. Working directly on these and other efforts will be Susan Stilman, our new Director of Corporate Educational Programs.

Through the program starting this fall in Executive Management for Women, Central will also serve as a direct bridge connecting corporations with a largely untapped pool of talent: the suburban housewife or lower-level company employee with a college background dating back a decade or more who needs up-to-date credentials and skills to qualify for management positions. Because of our long and splendid history as a women's college we have a special obligation to contribute in this regard to the advancement of women. And our extensive involvement in encouraging mature women to return to the classroom and in helping them achieve a rewarding education has given us the experience needed to make such a program work. We believe all this will produce a splendid partnership among women, higher education, and the corporate community.

This past year, other types of community outreach programs also flourished at the College. In a unique cooperative effort with Boston University, two distinguished B.U. graduate schools began offering advanced degrees at Central in biology, physics, and business. The response so far has been encouraging, and even more interest should be generated when three additional master's degrees—in art history, political science, and economics—are brought to the campus this fall.

Apart from helping us serve the community, this relationship with a forward-looking, diversified university has tangible benefits for our own undergraduates. Qualified upperclassmen have access to these graduate courses, which give them an excellent advantage in applying to graduate or professional school, as well as preparation for a career. In addition, a cooperative program permits students to earn both a Central degree and an MBA from B.U. in five years. A similar program should start in September 1991, joining undergraduate philosophy and liberal arts with graduate study in psychology.

Meanwhile, B.U.'s International Cultural Institute (ICI), which began on our campus this spring, should help us attract more undergraduates from foreign lands who are qualified academically, but require some intensive language training. A nationally renowned program in English as a Second Language, the ICI blends well into the substance and fiber of Central. Next semester, 8 percent of our entering freshman class will come from other lands, continuing the tradition of welcoming international students which stretches back to our days as an Institute. In fact, our curriculum was among the nation's first to recognize the need for an academic approach to other lands and cultures. More than a decade ago, an Eastern European Studies program began at the College, joined later by ones in Middle Eastern Studies and African Studies and three years ago, by a new major in Slavic Languages.

Continuing this pattern, the faculty this spring established a new major in International Studies, which will draw upon existing courses in language, politics, economics, and area studies. Through this program, our students will explore supranational problems and issues, such as the energy crisis, preservation of the environment, monetary and trade policy, and human rights. Coordinating this new major is a faculty committee, chaired by Rhee Ha Lim, Professor of Economics. Mr. Lim, by the way, was recently invited by the Woodson National Scholars to participate in a study group on U.S.—China relations, consisting of 20 persons drawn from universities, business, journalism, and the legislative and executive branches of government.

Many others in our faculty have been equally active this year as scholars and authors. French Professor Jeannette Meure, for instance, received an America Philosophical Society grant for study of ''The French Rationalists in Lyon in the Eighteenth Century,'' while James Goodwin joins the faculty of Studenbaker College in New York during his leave next year.

In the English Department, Professor Elaine Husting was awarded a travel grant by the English Speaking Union to work in Oxford this summer, completing research for another of her books. And JoAnn J. Zimmer, in addition to serving as chairperson of our Linguistics Department, is an editorial advisor for Lingua Nova, a new journal for the study of classical linguistics.

Retiring from the faculty this spring after many years of dedicated service were noted journalist Jacob Erickson and Ethel Morris of the German Department and Edith Williams, Professor of Psychology. Professor Richard Steed also retired from full-time teaching, but will return this fall on a part-time basis. While not retiring, Rose Marie Woodson has left the college to accompany her husband to Kansas, where he is completing his doctorate. Replacing her as Director of Community Studies is Linda Paxton. I know you all share with me the deep gratitude felt by the College community for their talents as teachers and for the many productive lives they have helped shape, and wish them well in the years to come.

On the administrative side of things, there are some changes, too. Smith Porter, who has contributed much to the College since he joined our faculty in 1967, resigned his position as Registrar and, after his sabbatical in the spring semester, will return to the Classics Department in fall of 1992. His duties as Registrar have been absorbed by other members of the Administrative Committee. In the Library, Mary O'Hara of the History Department agreed to serve as the new Director when Harold Charles resigned to take a position with the Library of Congess in Washington.

Students were also active this year, displaying promising leadership qualities which certainly bode well for the future. Of the three candidates who ran for President of Student Government last spring, two were sophomores; the sophomore who won, Greg Michaels, is a member of our first B.A./M.B.A. class (the new cooperative program with Central University Business School enabling students to earn both degrees in a time-shortened sequence which integrates study of business and the liberal arts).

As we conclude our farewells to the Class of 1990 our thoughts are very much with these entering students, the Class of 1994, and with our plans for the new academic year—not that the summer is quiet on campus, just somewhat different. At Commencement ceremonies on Sunday, May 25, we were honored by the presence of two Honorary Degree recipients: former Lauenbach College president David White and Amantha Sethwaite, widow of former Congressman Jonathan Sethwaite, who has been loyal to the College ever since she studied for a time with the Class of 1938. A longtime friend of Central (the alma mater of several of his family), Mr. White offered a thoughtful Commencement address, which I know the graduating class found to be particularly pertinent to their own futures, both as individuals and as responsible members of our society. Two days after Commencement, on Tuesday, May 27, the schedule of summer classes began with four different sessions and over 100 courses in more than 20 different fields. Continuing this busy pace, summer sessions end on Wednesday, August 20, and registration for the 1990—91 academic year starts on Wednesday, September 10!

I hope you will agree that the 1989—90 year has been marked by much progress both academically and financially, and in the spiritual, as well as intellectual character of the College. In particular, we were delighted at the excellent response we received from all of you in support of matching funds under our Ford Foundation Grant, which resulted in the largest annual fund in the history of the College—truly a remarkable record. We recognize, however, that the next two years of the grant will pose even more of a challenge, since additional matching funds become available. We are making plans now not only to continue this kind of achievement but actually to surpass it. Once the fall semester gets underway, it will be my pleasure to write to you once again and bring you up—to—date on our progress.

Lydia Brinton Carlton

WHAT TO DO

Yes, this is a *real* college newsletter. You probably receive several similar ones every year from schools, nonprofit organizations, civic clubs, and businesses that pride themselves on community involvement.

A literate, caring person has gathered a lot of information and talked it into a tape recorder, leading the reader down a meandering lane of news and thoughtful observations. Unfortunately, only the most dedicated readers are likely to make the time to stroll along with such writing. Most readers are pressed for time and want to know "what's new?"

1. Make a pencil slash wherever the writer changes the subject.

2. Suggest a heading for each section in the margin of the Original.

3. Underline the information in each section that the reader needs to know.

WHAT WE DID

OUR REWRITE

Headings help pull your readers and give them an overview. The use of headings is also invaluable to *you* when you are crafting your first draft.

We have created headings and internal lists so the readers can scan the entire letter looking for "what's new?" and familiar names.

CENTRAL COLLEGE

July 1990

Dear Alumni, Parents, and Friends

We were delighted at the excellent response we received from all of you for matching funds for our Ford Foundation grant. Your gifts resulted in the largest annual fund in the history of the College. We are making plans now to not only continue this record, but to actually surpass it, as additional matching funds become available.

In the past year, we've made remarkable progress in other areas as well—in our financial position, as an important intellectual resource for the surrounding community, and as a community of scholars, students, and individuals.

Financial Stability

After a year of negotiation, the College sold 23.4 acres of surplus property to the Spector Company. This step was essential not only to the College, putting it on a sound financial footing, but also to the economic future of Sussex County. This sale eliminated 50% of our accumulated deficit. Without it, our long-term viability would have been in serious question.

Community Outreach

Recent years have seen extensive changes in the Macklin/Devon/Essex/Newtown area, as several major firms have relocated their corporate headquarters. I firmly believe that working with these companies is an important part of the College's mission. We are planning some exciting co-operative ventures:

- a program of work opportunities and internships for our undergraduates, more and more of whom are choosing business as a career,
- an exchange program between corporate personnel and our faculty, and
- a re-entry program for women who need to update their academic credentials to qualify for management positions.

New Academic Programs

During the past year, we offered advanced degrees in biology, physics, and business through Boston University. This fall we will offer master's degrees in art history, political science and economics, also through B.U. Another program with B.U. will permit students to earn a five year MBA, integrating the study of business and liberal arts.

The International Cultural Institute of B.U., whose English as a Second Language program is nationally known, will help us attract more undergraduates from abroad. This will complement our established curriculum in Eastern European Studies, Middle Eastern Studies, African Studies, and Slavic Languages.

This spring the faculty established a new major in International Studies, which will draw upon existing courses in language, politics, economics, and area studies.

Faculty Achievements

JoAnn J. Zimmer, Chairperson of Linguistics, is an editorial advisor for Lingua Nova, a new journal for the study of classical linguistics.

Elaine Husting, Professor of English, was awarded a travel grant by the English Speaking Union to work in Oxford this summer. She will complete research for another book.

Jeannette Meure, Professor of French, received an American Philosophical Society grant for study of ''The French Rationalists in Lyon in the Eighteenth Century.''

Rhee Ha Lim, Professor of Economics, is a member of a study group on U.S.-China relations sponsored by the Woodson National Scholars. He is also chair of the faculty committee which will coordinate the new International Studies major.

James Goodwin, Psychology, joins the faculty of Studenbaker College in New York during his leave next year.

Administrative Changes

Smith Porter has resigned as Registrar and will return to his position in the Classics Department in fall, 1991, after a sabbatical during the spring semester. His duties have been absorbed by other members of the Administrative Committee. Mary O'Hara, History Department, is the new Director of the Library.

et cetera . . .

CHAPTER 16

Notifications

There are two kinds of notifications: everyday ones and urgent ones. We'll deal with the ultimate Perfect Letter challenge, the "Urgent Notification," at the end of this book.

Everyday notifications—when you want to remind people about something you've already told them or let them know about something new that may (or may not) interest them—should still be as easy to read as life-or-death messages. Use all your Perfect Letter skills to polish the real notification letters on the following pages.

SPECTOR WORLD ENTERPRISES

May 20, 1997

Mr. Graham Chapman
Omega Electronics
111 Cleese Place
Spectorville, CA 94117

Dear Mr. Chapman:

The National Electronics in Medicine Symposium will be held on Saturday, June 15, at the Civic Auditorium from 9:00 a.m. to 4:00 p.m. The conference will be attended by approximately 500 medical and electronics leaders from six western states.

The format of the workshop is loosely based on the AMME national conference, with a variety of sessions being offered throughout the day in the areas of dialysis, cochlear implants, defibrillation units, CAT-SCANS, etc.

As our opening speaker, you will start the day off at 9:00 a.m. and have approximately 45 minutes to speak. The topic of your speech is your choice, but since 90 percent of all the leaders at the training will be attending an electronics-medicine oriented conference for the first time, we would appreciate it if you would touch on the importance of maintaining constant communication between the engineering and medical professions.

I will have a check for you in the amount of $1500.00 on the day of the workshop, and you are cordially invited to spend the rest of the day with us, and be our guest for lunch.

I am enclosing the registration flyer that was sent to participating hospitals and medical centers. I will send you a map of the city and a narrative description of each session as soon as I get them back from the printers.

The workshop committee is very pleased you agreed to be our speaker and we look forward to seeing you on the fifteenth.

If you have any questions, please call me at (1-415) 555-9876.

Sincerely,

Michael Paien
Symposium Coordinator

Wнат то DO

Yes, this is a real letter! Imagine that you are sending this information to a busy executive who has agreed to speak at this symposium. How do you help him to show up at the right place at the right time?

1. The information about time and place is where it should be, in the first paragraph. How could you make it more readable and more specific for the reader?

2. Suggest headings that will help the reader through the information in this letter.

3. The spacing of this Original is cramped and makes it very difficult to read. How can you improve the layout?

Wʜᴀᴛ ᴡᴇ ᴅɪᴅ

ANSWERS

1. Whenever you are notifying someone about a meeting schedule, it helps to "break out" the information from the text, centering the date, time, and place on separate lines. That way it is nearly impossible to miss and easily retrievable. For example:

Monthly Planning Meeting
Tuesday, May 18
2:00 ᴘ.ᴍ.
Room 702

2. We have used headings in the Rewrite to help the reader scan the information.

3. Use indents, highlights, and spacing as you use emphasis and pauses in speech.

REWRITE

SPECTORVILLE ASSOCIATION

May 20, 1997

Mr. Graham Chapman
Omega Electronics
111 Cleese Place
Spectorville, CA 94117

Dear Mr. Chapman:

You are scheduled to open the Western Electronics in Medicine Symposium:
Saturday, June 15
Civic Auditorium
9:00 A.M.
You will have approximately 45 minutes to speak. You are cordially invited to spend the rest of the day with us and to be our guest for lunch. The symposium ends at 4:00 P.M.

Speech Topic: The choice is yours, but we would appreciate it if you would touch on the importance of maintaining constant communication between the engineering and medical professions.

Workshop Format: It will be loosely based on the AMME national conference, with a variety of sessions being offered throughout the day in the areas of dialysis machines, cochlear implants, defibrillation units, CAT-SCANS, etc. Approximately 500 medical and electronics leaders from six western states have registered. Ninety percent are attending a combined electronics-medicine conference for the first time.

Driving Directions: I will send you a map of Spectorville (and a symposium schedule) as soon as they are back from the printer.

Payment: I will have your check for $1500.00 on the day of the workshop.

The workshop committee is very pleased you have agreed to be our speaker and we look forward to seeing you on the fifteenth. If you have any questions, please call me at (1-415) 555-9876.

Sincerely,

Michael Palen
Symposium Coordinator

Encl: Registration flyer

SPECTOR EXPORT SERVICES

March 14, 1997

Ms. Emily West
MacDonald Electronics
799 Raymond Avenue
Eddy, IL 59980

                    SUBJECT: Canadian Orders when the
                             destination is not Canada

Dear Ms. West:

All electronic products manufactured by MacDonald Electronics can be
shipped directly to Canada under a G—Dest license. That is true if it is
Department of Commerce or Department of State licensable.

When the ultimate destination is not Canada, as is the case with products
started in the United States and finished in Canada for return to this
country or for sale abroad, then the end destination and end use must be put
on the ELB order form by the Canadian Sales Office. An individual export
license must be obtained for any country other than Canada. A complete and
full disclosure of all particulars is necessary to obtain the export
licenses, and we need to be aware of this at the time of the order entry. If
this information is not given initially, then at the time the ship—to
address is cleared, I would have to apply for the license. This could cause a
great delay in delivery.

Please call me if you have any questions on Canadian orders that will need
this type of license.

Sincerely,

Zack Brown
International Shipping

What to do

The writer's opening sentence reflects the starting point of his thinking about this situation. Does it position the readers and tell them why he is writing?

1. Underline the sentence that describes the purpose of the letter.
2. Put a check next to anything the readers can do to avoid this problem.
3. Suggest a new opening sentence that positions the readers about the problem and potential solutions.

WHAT WE DID

ANSWERS

1. The purpose of this letter is in the next to last sentence: "This could cause a great delay in delivery."

2. The things the readers can do to avoid this problem are highlighted in the Rewrite.

3. A new opening sentence that positions the readers about the problem and potential solutions is: "You can avoid long delays in delivery of your Canadian shipments if you will notify me immediately when you make an order entry for shipment of a Canadian order with a non-Canadian destination."

OUR REWRITE

SUBJECT changed from:

Canadian Orders when the destination is not Canada

to:

How to avoid shipping delays on Canadian orders

SPECTOR EXPORT SERVICES

March 14, 1997

Ms. Emily West
MacDonald Electronics
799 Raymond Avenue
Eddy, IL 59980

SUBJECT: <u>How to avoid shipping delays on</u>
<u>Canadian orders</u>

Dear Ms. West:

You can avoid long delays in delivery if you will notify me immediately whenever you make an order entry for shipment of a Canadian order with a non-Canadian destination.

All products manufactured by MacDonald Electronics are government-licensable, so orders going on from Canada to other countries or returning to the United States need separate licensing.

<u>To ship elsewhere on Canadian orders</u>

1. Be sure the Canadian Sales Office has filled in ''end destination'' and ''end use'' on the ELB order form.
2. Notify me immediately when you enter the order.
3. Include a complete and full disclosure of product and final destination so I can obtain the necessary export licenses. (If I wait to apply for the licenses until the ship-to address is cleared, there can be a big delay.)

<u>To ship directly to Canada</u>

No problem—we can use our G-Dest license.

Please call me at 1-800-555-8888, ext. 721, if you have any questions.

Sincerely,

Zack Brown
International Shipping

Your Perfect Letter Checklist

☑ **AVOID JARGON**

It's tempting to show how aware you are—how hep, hip, cool, groovy, hot, boss, bad, fly—by using the latest slang. But as you can see, nothing dates faster than the latest buzz words. When you are writing formal letters or any letter you hope will be on record for some time to come, pretend that your reader is hopelessly square and use standard English. Save the hot new vernacular for special occasions.

If you are writing to someone outside your profession, check that none of the common trade terms you are used to using will be misunderstood by the reader. Resist the temptation to show off your knowledge of technical terms unless you are trying to confuse and intimidate your reader. (Which, of course, a Perfect Letter never does!)

Imagine receiving letters with sentences like these:

- "Assuming *arguendo* that we can still establish *personam jurisdiction*, your *trespasse quare clausum fregit* is *res ipsa loquitur*."
- "We have finished the type specing. The blue lines should be in your hands by the first of the month."
- "The poor fit in your seconds was caused by a defective marker combined with a gray-goods problem."

Each of these statements is intelligible to someone in the business. When you talk to someone *out* of the business, don't lose business by using business jargon.

CHAPTER 17

Promotional Letters

The subject of "direct mail" promotional letters could and does fill dozens of books, so we're not going to offer comprehensive instructions for competing with national specialists in this art form. However, your department, organization, or small business may want to promote itself, a special activity, or a new offer without hiring an advertising agency.

How do you go about it? Look at the following real examples to discover some pitfalls you can easily avoid.

SUPERSUPPORT SYSTEMS

December 21, 1999

Dear Vera Bromley:

Enclosed, you will find our reference sheet and our company's initial advertisement, which will give you a brief idea about who we are and what we do.

We have recently received our Service Part Ordering Number from IBM which enabled us to engage in the complete service and repair of the IBM PCs. Our services are provided on site. Services and repairs are done on a time-and-material basis.

Our basic rates are as follows:

Minimum (includes first two hours)	$ 50.00
Every hour thereafter	$ 30.00
Travel to customer site and back	$ .20/mile

Hour starts when technician leaves depot and ends when he returns.

Our response time for most service calls is one day. Turnaround time for damaged assemblies depends on the severity of the problem. However, in the very near future, we will be providing Flat Exchange Rates on specific assemblies (i.e. Disk drives, Monitor, CPU board, etc.) which means that you will get faster service and won't have to wait for the turnaround of assemblies.

We provide Preventive Maintenance (PVM) at your request. I strongly recommend PVMs at least twice a year, even if system is hardly ever used.

We provide our services at your convenience. We can also be reached after hours and on weekends.

Please feel free to call me if I can be of any help.

Sincerely,

Michael Knowles, Partner

WHAT TO DO

The writer thinks the "news" is that his firm just received an IBM Service Part Ordering Number. But what is probably the real news for the reader?

1. Put a check next to each feature or benefit the writer is offering. Which one is probably the most appealing to the reader? (This should be first in the letter.)

2. Suggest a heading for each subject.

WHAT WE DID

ANSWERS

1. The most appealing benefit the writer is offering is probably the long hours and on-site availability of service.

2. Compare your suggested headings to those in our Rewrite.

SUPERSUPPORT SYSTEMS

December 21, 1999

Dear Vera Bromley:

We'd like to introduce ourselves and our SuperSupport Services for all your microcomputer needs.

Service when you need it
We are ready to serve you at <u>your</u> convenience at <u>your</u> location. And you can reach us at any time—after hours and on weekends too!

NEW—IBM PC services
We recently received our Service Part Ordering Number from IBM so we can now offer complete service and repair of IBM PCs, in addition to Apple, Macintosh, Compaq, and Corona.

Unbeatable rates
Compare our rates for all our full support services:

Minimum (includes first two hours)	$ 50.00
Every hour thereafter	$ 30.00
Travel to customer site and back	$ .20/mile

Time charges start when technician leaves our Spectorville depot and end when he returns. Services and repairs are done on a time—plus—materials basis.

Fast response time
Our response time for most service calls is one day. Turnaround time for damaged assemblies depends on the severity of the problem. In the very near future we will be providing flat exchange rates on specific assemblies (i.e., disc drives, monitors, CPU boards, etc.), which means even faster turnarounds on assemblies.

Preventive maintenance
We strongly recommend that you use our Preventive Maintenance (PVM) at least twice a year to keep costly problems from developing. PVM is especially important if the system is used infrequently.

Call us. We want to help.

Sincerely,

Michael Knowles, Partner

Encl: Reference sheet
      Advertising tearsheet

DYNAMICS UNLIMITED, LTD.

Sam Samson
Sally Samson
Bill Strong

December 23, 1998

Season's Greetings:

I have been, on the whole, dissatisfied for the last few years with the quality of the outcomes achieved in training both in IPD and Utilization. My perception is that this has occurred for two reasons:

1. The training conducted has been in association with other organizations (e.g., Incorporated Power, Inc.) and other individuals (e.g., Atlas) whose outcomes and conduct did not always coincide with mine.

2. The incomplete and sporadic nature with which the technology developed initially by Johnson and myself has been applied to the teaching/training of the technology.

To correct this situation, I have taken several steps:

1. I am now conducting certification training in IPD through Dynamics Unlimited, Ltd. (003/433-7244) under the auspices of the Society of Interpersonal Power Dynamics, independently of Incorporated Power, Inc. and Utilization, Inc. This allows me full quality control over the training I conduct. This partially addresses the first difficulty noted above.

2. I have worked hard over the last months on a systematic application of the technology itself.

Specifically, in the area of business consulting and training, I am offering a completely new apprenticeship program. This program, while not fully explicated, has the following structure:

1. A new 24-day program broken into three 8-day sections with a minimum of 3 months (90 days) for consolidation/integration between each segment.

2. A stronger physical component to the training (principle-physiology leads behavior), including a challenging set of outdoor individual and leadership tasks.

3. Explicit training using technology to train people in the technology.

4. The incorporation of all the new material (e.g. quality circles, moments of excellence, training and the outdoor challenge events, platform skills, negotiation, and mediation).

The program will be conducted completely under my quality control. At the end of the 24-day schedule, I will determine which of the participants, if any, meet my criteria for excellence in business consulting and training. When a participant has qualified through this program, he or she will receive a Qualification of Excellence as a business consultant/trainer. This document will be executed by me personally. This Qualification of Excellence as a business consultant/trainer means I will personally guarantee this person's performance. Thus I place my personal and professional competencies behind them. If, for example, in servicing a contract reviewed by me for a corporation, the corporation is not satisfied with the outcome, I will service that contract to client satisfaction personally. I wish to point out unequivocally that for me to extend this performance guarantee—that is, for me to award the Qualification of Excellence as a business consultant/trainer—will require the person awarded it to meet the highest quality standards during training; they must meet my subjective perceptual standards for excellence. Any person, therefore, entering this program must recognize that there is no guarantee of such an award, only a guarantee of the highest quality training I personally can generate.

At the conclusion of the 24 days, a roster with a maximum of 20 names will be compiled, listing those who have, in my opinion, achieved the highest degree of excellence. The trainers on this roster will be selected on a rotating basis to fulfill contracts awarded from businesses to Sam Samson.

The first 8-day segment of the 24-day program will be conducted on March 4-11 in Spectorville. The seminar will be conducted by me with the assistance of Ali Kelly and Simon Ford. The cost for the 8 days will be $900.00.

I realize that there is a group of people who have already trained in IPD and have been awarded the Practitioner Certification who are interested in business practice as well. Recognizing this, I am offering a 4-day abbreviated version of the first 8-day segment—the cost is $600 (dates March 8-11) for people who already have a Practitioner Certificate in IPD. Please note that acceptance in this first segment does not guarantee an invitation to the second segment of the 24-day program (to be conducted in either August or October), only, as I stated, the highest quality training I can conduct.

If interested, send an application plus a deposit of $400.00 for the 8-day training or $200.00 for the 4-day training to:

> March Seminar
> 221 J. Street
> Central City, WI

For additional information, you may phone 003/666-3333.

Sam Samson

WHAT TO DO

This *real* (but carefully disguised) letter was sent by a person who sells communications workshops! How do you rate him as a communicator?

Apparently, he is distressed that others, possibly even a former partner, have begun teaching his technique. He wants to regain control of the market. This letter represents the Exploratory Phase of his thinking about the problem. He belittles his competitors, repeats some information several times, and offers several addresses and phone numbers where he can be reached. Are you tempted to contact him?

1. Did the writer aim this letter at potential workshop participants or at potential employers of trained candidates?

   ( ) workshop particpiants

   ( ) employers

   ( ) both

2. Find the "news" and underline it. What does the reader need to know?

3. Circle any information that could be transferred to an accompanying brochure or application form—details that may keep the letter from being easily understood, but which would be interesting if the reader wants to know more.

WHAT WE DID

ANSWERS

1. The writer seems to be trying to talk to both potential workshop participants and employers. Two separate letters would be better, but we have crafted one to do double duty.

2. The "news" is scattered throughout the three pages:

    "I am now conducting certification training in IPD. . . ."

    "A new 24-day program broken into three 8-day sections . . ."

    "When a participant has qualified through this program. . . . I will personally guarantee this person's performance."

    "If . . . the corporation is not satisfied with the outcome, I will service that contract to client satisfaction personally."

    "The trainers . . . will be selected on a rotating basis to fulfill contracts. . . ."

    "The first 8-day segment of the 24-day program will be conducted on March 4–11 in Spectorville. . . . $900.00."

3. The letter would be more forceful and easier to read if details about the workshops, applications, assistants, and deposits were in an accompanying brochure.

OUR REWRITE

We have added a headline: "Certification for IPD Instructors." The purpose—announcing the certification program and resulting job opportunities—is now in the opening paragraph. The other news is highlighted with headings.

The Original was mass-printed without any salutation. We've done a version with a computer-inserted personalized greeting.

We've also removed all those alternate addresses and phone numbers—they make Mr. Samson appear unorganized or unreliable.

DYNAMICS UNLIMITED, LTD.

Sam Samson
Sally Samson
Bill Strong
December 23, 1998

Mr. John Randolph
The Selwyn Corporation
2395 First Avenue
Central City, WI 00888
<u>Certification for IPD Instructors</u>

Dear John:

I have decided to personally supervise certification of IPD instructors through the Society of Interpersonal Power Dynamics (SIPD). I will then refer all contracts to teach Interpersonal Power Dynamics to these certified practitioners on a rotating basis.

In the seven years since I developed Interpersonal Power Dynamics with Carl Johnson, it has been my pleasure to see it accepted as a major innovation among training and personnel directors. Unfortunately, its success has also meant a rash of imitators and well-intentioned former students of mine who try to implement and teach the system without adequate background or expertise.

<u>My Personal Performance Guarantee</u>: The men and women who complete a 24-day training program under my direction and who, in my highly subjective opinion, become experts in Interpersonal Power Dynamics will receive SIPD certification and my personal guarantee:

> They will service training contracts to the client's complete satisfaction or I will personally finish the job.

<u>My New Training Program</u>: The first of three 8-day sessions is:

> March 4-11
> Central City Motor Lodge
> Cost: $900

> (A 4-day session for those already certified by the SIPD will be offered March 8-11 for $600.)

> For more information give me a call.

Cordially,

Sam Samson
Encl: application form

Your Perfect Letter Checklist

☑ **AVOID BE'S—USE DIRECT SENTENCES**

"To be" is the most conjugated verb in the English language, but try to avoid "be" in letters—or at least verb constructions that substitute "be" for direct, active, transitive verbs.

Passive	*Active*
should be done	please do
	tell me who will do
must be completed	complete by (date)
action should be taken	take action by (date)
should be discussed	Let's discuss Thursday
should be soon	Call me no later than Tuesday if you cannot fill my order by May 10

CHAPTER 18

Refusals

Turning someone down is rarely easy. That's why so many refusal letters are so bad. Two temptations exist:

1. Reject the reader as simply and briefly as possible, citing company policy or rules or some other outside and uncontrollable force. This may save time but can create ill will that comes back to haunt the writer or company years later in unexpected ways.

2. Try to phrase the refusal so diplomatically that the reader is unsure what is being said and may feel that promises have been made or real hope has been offered. This can also have serious future repercussions.

When you must refuse, be clear, be direct, and be kind. Consider whether the readers may have any emotional involvement in a refusal. Are they likely to see it as a personal rejection instead of random chance or the result of unrelated events? Can you soften this, even hint that the deficiency is in you, not the reader?

Even an impersonal refusal—"Sorry, we don't carry red wool socks"—can be turned into a positive, business-enhancing Perfect Letter by adding a few more words: "We have red polyester or navy wool if either would suit your needs. However, I believe the Williams Sock Company in Topeka may offer red wool. Their toll-free order number is 1-800 MY SOCKS." Instead of just getting one more annoying piece of paper off your desk (the query letter), you have turned a prospect into a friend by proving a valuable ally in the quest for perfect socks.

SPECTORVILLE BANK

March 28, 1998

Ms. Susan McGovern
1536 Mission St.
San Francisco, CA 94105

Dear Ms. McGovern:

Your resume and inquiry about the position of personnel manager at Spectorville Bank has been received as of March 8, 1998.

We find no immediate opening for someone with your skills.

Please be aware that all resumes are maintained in our files for three years, according to our policy. We are an equal opportunity employer and sensitive to the diversity in our community.

All resumes are reviewed whenever an opening occurs. Be sure that your resume will be taken into consideration when an opening occurs in your field.

Thank you very much for contacting Spectorville Bank.

Sincerely,

Sheila FitzPatrick
Employment Manager

WHAT TO DO

This letter concentrates too much on the bank's system and compliance with the law. It sounds like it's saying, "Please don't sue us."

1. Cross out any information that the reader probably doesn't need or want to know.
2. Underline the "news."
3. Suggest some ways to soften the letter and make it more congenial.

WHAT WE DID

ANSWERS

1. The reader probably doesn't need or want to know:

   - that the bank has received her resume (obviously it has)
   - that they maintain files for three years
   - that they are an Equal Opportunity Employer (most likely this is required by federal, state, or local law)
   - that they are sensitive to the diversity of the community (such sensitivity should be reflected in their refusal letters)

2. The "news" is that they have no job opening for the reader.

3. We have softened the letter by:

   - opening with a thank you
   - making a specific reference to the quality of the reader's credentials (This should be possible with nearly every job applicant—if not, the sentence could be dropped.)
   - wishing the job hunter luck
   - keeping the tone of the letter friendly and supportive of the job hunter in her search

SPECTORVILLE BANK

March 28, 1998

Ms. Susan McGovern
1536 Mission Street
San Francisco, CA 94105

Dear Ms. McGovern:

Thank you very much for your resume and inquiry about a position as personnel
manager at Spectorville Bank.

Your credentials are certainly impressive. I've sent a copy of your resume
to the head of Human Resources Management, which supervises our Personnel
Department. Unfortunately we have no immediate opening for someone with
your skills.

We will keep your resume on file and contact you if anything changes. In the
meantime, the best of luck.

Sincerely,

Sheila FitzPatrick
Employment Manager

SPECTOR CORPORATION

January 12, 1994

Ms. Cynthia Chung, Director
Metropolitan Chinese Community Council
Employment and Training Program
111 Main Street
Central City, WI 90000

Dear Ms. Chung:

I have been informed that a funding proposal for your Employment and
Training Program will soon be considered and I would like to offer my
endorsement, at this time, of the efforts that the Metropolitan Chinese
Community Council has made towards establishing effective and meaningful
programs for the disadvantaged in your community.

I have been associated with M.C.C.C. for the past two years and have used
your employment service many times for bringing qualified candidates into
the workforce of Spector. Your clerical training program has been highly
successful in showing private industry that you can graduate clerical
applicants whose competency levels meet and often exceed the entry-level
requirements of our business world. My experience has been that not only do
your applicants meet the basic skills levels but they are also familiar with
good vocational English and are acculturated to the world of work so
necessary to being employed, remaining employed, and moving ahead.

I would also like to thank you for the continuing efforts you have shown in
involving individuals like myself in the design of your programs and
training materials and would like to again offer my support of your current
programs and any proposed programs of the future.

Because we have no openings at the present time, Spector cannot, at this
time, commit to any future hires, but it is my hope that M.C.C.C. will be able
to get the funding that it needs to expand its present operations and to
provide our company with more qualified entry-level and technical
applicants should we again request them.

Sincerely,

Sydney Ehrlich
Manager, Community Resources

WHAT TO DO

This writer had to deny a request for jobs while maintaining good relations with an outside training program. His solution was to offer lavish praise for three paragraphs and hide the bad news in the fourth paragraph.

1. What are the main purposes of this letter?

2. Suggest an opening that summarizes this.

3. Cross out any unnecessary or unfortunate language.

WHAT WE DID

ANSWERS

1. The writer wants to do two things:
    a. Tell the reader that there are no job openings right now.
    b. Provide a flattering letter that the reader can use as a fundraising tool.
2. Our opening paragraph accomplishes both these objectives.
3. We have deleted:

CLUMSY PHRASES

- "showing private industry that you can" (if you can, you can)
- "meet and often exceed the entry-level requirements" (the sentence following that one says it better)
- "being employed, remaining employed, and moving ahead" ("moving ahead" includes the first two concepts)

UNNECESSARY PHRASES

- "individuals such as myself"
- "the efforts that M.C.C.C. has made toward establishing"
- "bringing qualified candidates into the workforce of Spector"
- "my experience has been that"
- "proposed programs of the future"

DEMEANING PHRASES

- "disadvantaged" (Crippled? Retarded? No, just untrained!)
- "our business world" (who is the "us" of "our"?)
- "acculturated to the world of work" (are hard workers rare in the Chinese community?)
- "future hires" (personnel jargon)

SPECTOR CORPORATION

January 12, 1994

Ms. Cynthia Chung, Director
Metropolitan Chinese Community Council
Employment and Training Program
111 Main Street
Central City, WI 90000

Dear Ms. Chung:

Your program has been doing a great job! Although Spector has no job openings right now and isn't able to promise that we will have openings for your trainees in the near future, we want to endorse your excellent training and employment program. You certainly deserve to get the funding you need to expand your present operations.

In the two years that I have been associated with the Metropolitan Chinese Community Council, I have used your employment services many times. Your clerical training program has been highly successful. Your applicants meet and often exceed our entry-level requirements. They are also familiar with good vocational English and they have the incentive to move ahead in the business world.

It has been my pleasure to participate with other members of the business community in the design of your programs and training materials. Again, I offer my support of your current work and any future programs.

Sincerely,

Sydney Ehrlich
Manager, Community Resources

Your Perfect Letter Checklist

☑ **BREAK OUT IMPORTANT INFORMATION**

When you want something to stand out in a letter, put white space around it and center it on a line by itself. This is especially effective with date–time–place information for meetings, but you can also use it to highlight model or purchase order numbers, new telephone numbers, changes of address, new personnel, or any other subject you want the reader to notice.

CHAPTER 19

Response Letters

Answering questions and queries is often done with form letters. The danger is that in worst-case scenarios, a customer who has asked or complained about one thing will get a form explanation for another. This has probably happened to you. How did you feel? Frustrated? Angry? After all, you took your good time to *write*. Surely someone at the other end could have bothered to *read* your letter.

Rule one for responses is to read the letter you are replying to carefully. Rule two is to personalize your reply whenever possible. *Not* with the computer gimmick of inserting the reader's name into the body of the text—that looks phony and condescending. Personalize your reply by addressing the *needs* of the reader.

SPECTOR INDUSTRIES

March 16, 1995

Ms. Linda Ferratti
Mars Manufacturing
123 Comet Blvd.
Anaheim, CA 90222

Dear Ms. Ferratti:

I am pleased to send you a copy of our latest catalog describing our
evaporative condensers and cooling towers. Here, too, is a copy of our
Installation, Operation, and Maintenance Manual.

Thanks for your inquiry, Ms. Ferratti. If you have any questions about our
equipment, please let us hear from you. We'd be happy to explain the features
that make it an outstanding value and the benefits that would solve your
cooling and evaporating problems.

Sincerely yours,

L. Guildemeister
Marketing Manager

WHAT TO DO

This letter is a response to a sales inquiry. Apparently the writer thinks Mars Manufacturing is a good prospect—note that an expensive manual is being sent along with the catalogue—yet the writer has not taken the extra minutes necessary to address the prospect's interests and needs. (In these days of word-processing, inserting someone's name in the middle of a sentence doesn't personalize a letter!)

1. Check any of the following additions that might make this letter more responsive to the reader:
    ( ) Information about other kinds of equipment offered
    ( ) A description of how this equipment has been improved
    ( ) A history of the writer's company, including awards and patents
    ( ) Names and phone numbers of businesses similar to the reader's that have bought and used this same equipment
    ( ) The latest price and delivery schedule

2. Underline the sentence that hints why the manual is being sent.

WHAT WE DID

ANSWERS

1. All the information in the checklist should be in the catalog, not the letter, if they are important selling points. The only item that would be responsive to the interests of the reader would be:

   ``Names and phone numbers of businesses similar to the reader's that have bought and used this same equipment''

   Use your computers to insert customized marketing information, not just insert prospect's name in the middle of sentences.

2. Sending an installation and maintenance manual in response to a sales inquiry *might* be done:

   ``. . . because I suspect you will need a more detailed picture of how the evaporative condensers and cooling towers will interact with your present system.''

OUR REWRITE

We have added a phone extension in the body of the letter and a list of enclosures at the end.

We *assume* that such a potentially large purchase will be followed up by a phone call or a personal visit.

SPECTOR INDUSTRIES

March 16, 1995

Ms. Linda Ferratti
Mars Manufacturing
123 Comet Blvd.
Anaheim, CA 90222

Dear Ms. Ferratti:

Thank you for your query. Here is a copy of our latest catalog describing our evaporative condensers and cooling towers.

I notice that Mars Manufacturing is fairly near several other manufacturing firms that have installed our systems. One especially, Mardikian Enterprises in Burbank, has used four of our cooling towers for the past five years. You may want to talk to Brad Bracker there about their experiences, both with improved quality control and cost/performance return. A list of addresses, phone numbers, and contact names is enclosed.

I'm also sending you our Installation, Operation and Maintenance Manual because I suspect you will need a more detailed picture of how the evaporative condensers and cooling towers will interact with your present system. You can call me at 323-4000, ext. 487, when you've had a chance to look it over. I am eager to answer your questions and to prepare you a savings estimate based on your requirements.

Sincerely yours,

L. Gildemeister
Marketing Manager

Encl:
    1995 catalog
    I-O-M Manual
    List of purchasers

THE BROADCASTING COMMISSION

January 26, 1995

Mr. Roberto Santa Cruz
111 E. 59th Street
New York, NY 10022

Dear Mr. Santa Cruz:

Thank you for writing to the Broacasting Commission. We receive
approximately 50,000 comments, inquiries, or complaints about broadcasting
each year, and we believe that as a taxpayer you will understand why we try to
reduce expenses by supplying a summary of some of the Commission's policies,
which we believe will answer many complaints and inquiries, including your
own.

We appreciate your interest in writing to us, and if you believe that the
material on the following pages does not adequately explain the
Commission's policies in the area of your concern, we will try to provide a
more specific answer.

Sincerely,

Soan Tang
Communications Officer

WHAT TO DO

An executive friend, irritated by what he considered persistent, unfair bias in TV news reporting, wrote a complaint to a public regulatory agency about the programs on his local station. In reply he received this letter.

Why such gross lack of tact? Why did they have to irritate the complainant (and they certainly did) by indicating that he was only one of 50,000 people they hear from each year? It's true—but why mention it at all. The letter was intended as an apology, but became a put-down.

See if you can rewrite this turn-down letter into a cooperative, problem-solving letter.

1. Cross out any information the reader does not need to know.

2. What is missing from the letter?

3. Suggest a way that this computerized letter could be *more* responsive to the reader rather than less.

WHAT WE DID

ANSWERS

1. The reader probably does not want to know how many letters the Commission receives. Since he has taken the time to write, he also may not appreciate being told that the government is saving money by not replying.

2. Missing from the letter are:

   • a procedure for writing for more information— the implication is that a follow-up inquiry would be answered with a duplicate of this form letter.

   • a list of enclosures

3. One of the advantages of a computerized letter is that it is relatively easy for the writer to include a customized list of enclosures. We have assumed that, since the writer has some way to specify enclosures before the letter is mailed, this capacity could be used to mention them within the letter.

THE BROADCASTING COMMISSION
1776 UNION STREET NW
WASHINGTON, DC 07642

January 26, 1995

Mr. Roberto Santa Cruz
111 E. 59th Street
New York, NY 10022

Dear Mr. Santa Cruz:

Thank you for writing to the Commission.

I am enclosing a summary of some of the Broadcasting Commission's policies,
which I believe cover all the points you asked about. You will be
particularly interested in Sections 6(a), 7, 8, 10, and 12.

If you have any further questions, I'll be happy to try to answer them. Write
me at the Washington D.C. address above.

Sincerely,

Soan Tang
Communications Editor

Encl:
Excerpts 1995 Policy Statement

Your Perfect Letter Checklist

☑ **USE LISTS WISELY**

Numbered items in letters provide strong visual interests, but use them wisely. It's tempting to make information look important by numbering it, but that can be a trap.

Be sure that all the items are related—all steps to be taken in that order, all enclosures, all changes in procedure, all actions decided on at a meeting. Be grammatically consistent. When you use a sentence fragment under one and a full sentence under another, starting one item with a verb, the next with a gerund, and the third with a noun, you sound confused and confuse your reader. And don't use more than one numerical list under one heading.

CHAPTER 20

Thank You's

Even something as innocuous and well-meant as a prompt thank-you letter can fail to serve its purpose if you are not responsive to the needs of the reader.

Ask yourself:

- Does my thank-you letter sound spontaneous and genuinely grateful or does it sound like it was a "duty" for me to write?

- Are there specific things I can praise, rather than generalities? Do I need to do any "research" by asking some questions or checking facts before writing?

- Is this letter likely to be seen by others? Do I need to change anything I've said because of that?

Perfect Letter thank you's are more than form letters. They know how to speak to the secret places in people's hearts, truthfully praising the qualities that others prize most in themselves.

What if the person you are thanking is a total stranger? Find something about what you're thanking them for that is admirable, notable, apt, charming, or indispensable to you, then praise that special quality.

SPECTOR REHABILITATION INDUSTRIES

February 11, 1997

Mr. Jack Seastrom
Community Services
800 Gordon Road
Atlanta, GA 39982

Dear Mr. Seastrom:

Thank you for your presentation to our group on Sunday.

We appreciate your taking the time to be with us and hope it was an enjoyable evening for you.

Enclosed is your honorarium for $50.

Sincerely,

Wayne Englund
Program Committee

WHAT TO DO

How can a simple thank-you letter be insulting?

The busy executive who received this (real!) thank-you letter had agreed to waive his usual four-figure speaker's fee to address an especially worthy nonprofit group. He paid his own airfare, gave up personal plans, and spent six hours travel time on a Sunday to reach the group's event.

His speech was a fantastic success. The audience received his ideas enthusiastically and gave him a standing ovation at the end. Several days later he still felt a glow about his efforts to help and about his contribution. Then he received this letter. Thud.

List at least three things the writer *could* have said:

1.

2.

3.

WHAT WE DID

ANSWERS

Among the things the writer could have said are:

1. Your presentation was enthusiastically received.
2. Thank you for going to so much trouble to get here.
3. Thank you for waiving your usual speaker's fee.
4. Your presentation was worth far more than $50.
5. You are a generous, talented, worthwhile person.

OUR REWRITE

We have tried to recreate the excitement of the audience at this event and then thanked the reader for creating it.

It was unnecessarily insulting to send a $50 speaking fee to someone who usually receives seventy times that much! It implies that his services were actually being paid for. Our Rewrite has tried (probably unsuccessfully) to cover that unfeeling gaff.

SPECTORVILLE REHABILITATION INDUSTRIES

February 11, 1997

Mr. Jack Seastrom
Community Services
800 Gordon Road
Atlanta, GA 39982

Dear Mr. Seastrom:

The applause and shouts of enthusiasm following your presentation last Sunday are still echoing through the hills here in Vermont. It was one of the most stirring presentations I've ever been privileged to hear and I am sure none of us will ever forget it.

We are even more grateful, knowing the sacrifices you made to get here. Your generosity with your time and compassion is even greater than your eloquence as a speaker.

I know you waived your usual $3500 speaker's fee, which we appreciate tremendously. We hope you will allow us to contribute $50 towards your considerable travel expenses—only a token, I know, but I will be grateful if you will do me the honor of accepting it. Of course, your contribution to our organization is priceless!

Sincerely,

Wayne Englund
Program Committee

Encl: $50 travel check

Your Perfect Letter Checklist

WRITE TO YOUR READERS' NEED TO KNOW

Whenever you aren't sure what to say or how to say it, think about your readers. Who are they? What do they *need* to know? What do they *want* to know? What do you feel they *should* know? What are they capable of understanding? What are you capable of expressing?

When your letter answers all these questions, it is a Perfect Letter.

CHAPTER 21

Urgent Notifications

Last but not least—urgent notifications. These are the screaming sirens and flashing red lights of the correspondence world. Here is where a Perfect Letter can literally become a life saver.

Urgent Perfect Letters don't have to alarm the reader with cries of disaster and doom. They get their strong message across by doing everything you have been doing in this workbook:

- Put your purpose up front.
- Use active action verbs.
- Use strong headings.
- Use short sentences and paragraphs.

Try your new Perfect Letter skills on these two real Original letters. Misreading the first letter will only cost the readers money and aggravation. Misreading the second may cost them their lives.

ORIGINAL

CITY OF SPECTORVILLE
PUBLIC WORKS DEPARTMENT

June 5, 1999

DEAR PROPERTY OWNER:

RE: SIDEWALK, CURB & GUTTER CONSTRUCTION AND TREE WORK

This is a secondary notification of the construction which will take place
to the sidewalk and/or curb in front of your property. You have been notified
of the specific work which will take place. In locations where the sidewalk
will be bowed or arced within the public right-of-way around trees,
sprinkler systems may be encountered. It is the property owner's
responsibility to move or repair the sprinkler system which may be affected
by construction.

The contractor, Babel Construction Company, will be removing and capping
irrigation systems which, if left intact, would be under the newly poured
concrete. All parts will be left with the property owner.

It is not possible for the City to match and repair the various irrigation
systems encountered. Many are obsolete or not working. Others were placed in
the public right-of-way without a permit. We are happy to repair the damaged
sidewalks and curbs and preserve as many trees as possible during the
construction. We will be planting trees which are more proper to the site and
not known to cause similar damages. However, we have no way to properly
handle the irrigation repairs.

The best method for repairing sprinkler systems may be to remove it prior to
the construction work and repair it when work is completed.

Thank you for your cooperation in contributing to a successful Sidewalk and
Tree Program. If you have any questions, contact us at 888-5432, ext. 134 or
789.

Sincerely,

LEMUEL GULLIVER   FLEUR COWLES
Project Engineer   Arborist

What to do

Imagine that you return home after a hard day and find this letter in your pile of mail. Do you immediately grasp the importance of what you are being told and/or asked to do? Or do you set it aside to figure out later?

This letter was sent out by the Public Works department of a middle-sized city to hundreds of homeowners. How many of them do you think understood what was happening? How many of them responded appropriately, saving time, money, grief, and lawsuits?

1. Put a check mark next to what the reader is being asked to do.

2. Suggest a new opening that alerts the readers to the "news."

3. What problems does the reader encounter in a search for the purpose of this letter?
   ( ) passive verbs
   ( ) purpose not in first sentence
   ( ) lack of good headings

WHAT WE DID

ANSWERS

1. The writer here never says directly what the reader is expected to do. Some clues are:

   "It is the property owner's responsibility to move or repair the sprinkler system which may be affected by construction."

   ". . . remove it prior to construction and repair it when work is completed."

2. One way to catch the attention of the reader with the "news" is shown opposite in the Rewrite.

3. The reader encounters *all* these problems while searching for the purpose of this letter.

   (X)   passive verbs

   (X)   purpose not in first sentence

   (X)   lack of good headings

OUR REWRITE

The news that this is a second notice is less important to the reader than the news about the sprinklers. To keep it from distracting the reader, we have moved it to form a bottom line.

REWRITE

CITY OF SPECTORVILLE
PUBLIC WORKS DEPARTMENT

June 5, 1999

Dear Property Owner:

IMPORTANT NOTICE: Do you have a <u>sprinkler system</u> between your house and the
                  street?

If so, it may need to be removed during the upcoming Sidewalk Repair and Tree
Program so it's not covered by new concrete.

<u>Which Sprinklers Will Be Affected</u>: Any located where the new sidewalk will
be bowed around trees in the public right-of-way.

<u>Your Responsibility</u>: You are responsible for removing your sprinkler system
before repairs begin. However, the contractor, Babel Construction Company,
is willing to remove all above-ground parts they find, cap the irrigation
system, and give you the parts. If you plan to replace your system
afterwards, you may prefer to do the job yourself.

<u>Why the City Can't Fix Sprinklers</u>: It is impossible to match parts for the
many different kinds of irrigation systems. Many are obsolete, not working,
and/or placed in the public right-of-way without a permit.

<u>What the City WILL do</u>: We will repair damaged sidewalks and curbs,
preserving as many trees as possible during construction. Some trees will be
replaced with new ones that don't cause root damage to sidewalks.

Thank you for your cooperation in contributing to a successful Sidewalk and
Tree Program. If you have any questions, contact us at 888-5432, ext. 134 or
789.

Sincerely,

LEMUEL GULLIVER   FLEUR COWLES
Project Engineer   Arborist

<u>2ND NOTICE: Sidewalk, Curb & Gutter Construction and Tree Work</u>

SPECTOR MOTORS OF AMERICA, INC.

SUBJECT: Recall Campaign

Dear Owner,

This notice is sent to you in accordance with the requirement of the National Traffic and Motor Vehicle Safety Act.

SPECTOR has determined that a defect which relates to motor vehicle safety exists in 1993 through 1996 model Santana and 1992 through 1996 Sequoia fuel-injected vehicles equipped with automatic transmission. Our records indicate that you're the owner of one of the vehicles owned.

We have found that the free movement of the accelerator cable connecting the automatic transmission level with the throttle housing in your car may become impaired and, under some conditions, cause loss of engine power or prevent the accelerator pedal from returning to a complete idle. This condition could affect your ability to control the vehicle and, with little or no warning, could result in an accident.

Prior to the time that your car is being corrected, we ask that you be alert to any abnormal throttle control operation. In the event that you should detect irregular pedal operation, please contact any authorized SPECTOR dealer immediately.

To eliminate the possible problem, the dealer will replace the accelerator cable on your vehicle with a newly designed cable and, in addition, check, lubricate and, where necessary, replace other components in the accelerator system.

An initial supply of replacement accelerator cables will be available at SPECTOR dealerships on May 18. The estimated time reasonably necessary to perform the required work will be up to one and a half hours and, of course, will be free of charge to you. Please make an appropriate appointment with the service manager of any authorized SPECTOR dealer. If the dealer fails or is unable to remedy the defect without charge within a reasonable amount of time, you may call or write to:

SPECTOR MOTORS
1111 Main Avenue
Center City, WI 60000

Attention: Mr. James Whitaker
              Technical Services Department
Telephone: (999) 555-8888

or

Administrator
National Highway Traffic Safety Administration
U.S. Department of Transportation
Washington, D.C. 20590

We regret any inconvenience this action may cause; nevertheless, we are confident you understand our interest in motor vehicle safety as well as your satisfaction with our product. We therefore urge you to promptly arrange for the necessary work to be done.

Sincerely,
SPECTOR MOTORS OF AMERICA, INC.

C.Z. Jamison, Manager, Technical Services

WHAT TO DO

This real letter isn't badly written—if the reader has a college education. There was no conscious effort to confuse the reader and the letter was sent in a red-bordered envelope that announced:

IMPORTANT
Motor Vehicle Recall Notification

Unfortunately, as the Government Accounting Office reported in a 1982 study, "Most U.S. adults (54 percent) read at or below the 11th grade level whereas recall letters in most instances are written at a college reading level."

One of the hardest things to do is write simply without "writing down" to the reader. That is why many written instructions fail to do their job. In a disaster no one has the time nor the inclination to decipher complex directions. Concise, easy-to-read language can literally be the difference between life and death.

1. Decide who needs to act in response to this letter. Circle the affected car models.

2. Put stars next to the things the affected readers are being asked to do.

3. Number these actions in order of importance.

4. What fears might keep the reader from responding? Jot them down here.

5. Suggest headings that will help the reader understand the letter more quickly.

WHAT WE DID

ANSWERS

1. We have highlighted the affected car models.
2. We have listed the things the affected readers should do.
3. For order of importance, see our Rewrite.
4. Readers may fear expense or being without their car. We have stressed "Free" and used a heading to address the time issue.
5. We have used headings to help the reader understand quickly:

   - You should
   - You will get
   - You will also get
   - How long will it take
   - If you have a problem